Tongue
Twisters

Tongue Twisters

Sexy Food from Bin 941 & Bin 942

Gord Martin
Chef & Owner

ARSENAL PULP PRESS

VANCOUVER

ARSENAL PULP PRESS
103 - 1014 Homer Street
Vancouver, B.C.
Canada V6B 2W9
arsenalpulp.com

The publisher gratefully acknowledges the support of the Government of Canada through the Book Publishing Industry Development Program for its publishing activities.

Design by Lisa Eng-Lodge
Production assistance by Judy Yeung
Edited by Melva McLean
Cover and interior photography by Hamid Attie
Cover design by Solo

Printed and bound in Canada

The author and publisher assert that the information contained in this book is true and complete to the best of their knowledge. All recommendations are made without guarantee on the part of the author and Arsenal Pulp Press. The author and publisher disclaim any liability in connection with the use of this information. For more information, contact the publisher.

National Library of Canada
Cataloguing in Publication Data

Martin, Gordon
  Tongue twisters : sexy food from bin 941 & bin 942 / Gord Martin.

  Includes index.
  ISBN 1-55152-149-0

  1. Cookery. I. Title.

TX714.M369 2003   641.5   C2003-911199-7

Table of Contents

Acknowledgments

I would like to thank all of my staff at Bin 941 and Bin 942 for their continued excellence in service and culinary expertise. Without the loyalty and dedication of my staff, this effort would not be possible. At the Bins, we are both a team and a family; a close knit clan driven by passion. To be sure, my eccentricities can be challenging to deal with; I am blessed and lucky to have such tenacious characters to stick by me and realize my dreams. Thanks to you all.

Special thanks to Tina Fineza, Chef, Bin 942; Alan Prokuski, Chef, Bin 941; Edward Perrow, Sommelier, Bin 941; Oscar Linassi, Operations Director, Bin 941/Bin 942.

This book is dedicated to James and Aileen Martin, for without them, I would not have been born.

Thanks to my extensive sunglass collection for making me look cool under pressure.

Introduction

Becoming a great cook comes from years of practical experience, trials, and tribulations. The essence of cooking is to derive the most from every ingredient: let them shine in all their glory, blending them together with a little know-how to come up with truly stunning new creations bursting with flavour. After all, the most interesting-looking or sounding dishes don't mean a lot if they don't have flavour.

The art of creating intriguing dishes is the art of tongue twisting, blending flavours that traditionally may not belong together. Creating bold new flavour combinations necessarily involves taking a journey on the modern spice route – Marco Polo in the twentieth-first century. I define my style of cooking as "cross-cultural cuisine." Much of my cooking is based on the combination of elements from the cooking cultures of Thailand, Mexico, France, Japan, India, Italy, and many others, in such a way that the dishes are influenced by these cuisines but at the same time are wholly their own.

These days it's easy to hop on an airplane to exotic locations and experience new taste sensations, but it's not entirely necessary. Travel to the ethnic districts in your city and you'll discover some of the wonderful ingredients and techniques I've included in this book. You'll also find yourself motivated to try other exciting new recipes using the spices you'll discover. Don't be afraid to experiment. Remember: recipes are only guidelines for your tastebuds. Let *Tongue Twisters* be your invitation to tempt the adventurous cook inside you.

The dishes I serve up in this book are interchangeable, of course, and you'll have fun mixing them up to create your own delectable menus. The important thing to remember is that your flavour combinations should be a balance of the four fundamental tastes: salty, sweet, sour, and spicy.

And remember that using salt does not mean a recipe must be salty in flavour. Salt is above all a flavour enhancer; used properly, it draws out the natural juices and flavours of proteins and vegetables. Break the habit of automatically salting and peppering your food on the plate. Taste it first. In my restaurants, food is seasoned completely while cooking, so salt and pepper is not to be found on the tables. Learn to develop a palate that lets the natural flavour of high-quality ingredients shine through. With such a palate, you will discover the beauty of food in its simplest and most natural state.

I hope that *Tongue Twisters* will help you explore the possibilities of taste and teach you that food is so much more than basic nourishment. It has texture and aroma in addition to taste, and eating well is, in a sense, an act of foreplay. The connection between food and sex is undeniable. So let your lips quiver, your palate salivate, your extremities tingle. Food is the fire of passion, compassion, and lust. Without food, there would be no desire.

With *Tongue Twisters* as your guide, you will create adventurous cross-cultural cuisine. Don't be intimidated. Be inspired. Get in the kitchen and turn on your burners. Get this book wet, get it dirty, let it catch it on fire.

Welcome to Flavourland.

cheers,

Gord Martin

Vancouver

October 2003

A Note on Beverage Pairings

The beverage pairings that are included with the recipes in *Tongue Twisters* are suggestions only. They will give you the option of enjoying "Old World" or "New World" wines. Many varietals are now produced in countries other than their own origins, so pick your favourite style. You'll want your wines to have good balance and display the natural characteristics of that varietal. You will be surprised how your favourite wine will taste completely different from one year to the next, and how that varietal will change in flavour from different vineyards and different geographic regions.

You may also be pleasantly surprised how a wine that has grown to become your favourite could get pushed to the back of the shelf after you experiment with that same varietal from a completely different region.

Remember: think regionally, drink globally.

GM

Basics

Crème Anglais

2¼ cups 2% milk

2¼ cups heavy or whipping cream

2 whole vanilla beans

10 egg yolks

1 cup white sugar

2 oz good quality single malt Scotch (optional)

Put egg yolks in a large mixing bowl. Add in sugar and blend with wooden spoon until smooth and fully incorporated; this procedure is called "creaming the egg."

In a heavy-bottomed stainless steel pot on medium heat, combine milk and cream. Cut vanilla beans lengthwise and scrape out seeds. Put seeds and pods into milk mixture. Let vanilla infuse on medium for about 10 minutes. Bring to boil.

Slowly, 1 oz at a time, ladle hot milk/cream into egg mix, stirring after 6 ladles have been added. Now, stirring constantly, pour in remaining milk. This is called "tempering the egg," so it won't scramble.

Pour mixture back into pot and add Scotch now if desired. Over medium-high heat, continue to cook, stirring, until mixture thickens. When you lift the spoon out of the mixture, the drips should form a little ribbon on top of mixture in pot. Another test is to scrape back of spoon with your fingernail. When done you should have a clean strip on spoon while the cream mixture adheres around it.

Remove from heat. Strain through a mesh strainer and let cool.

Place *crème Anglais* in fridge overnight. It can be used just like a classic dessert sauce for chocolate cake, etc. or to make ice cream (see page 186 for recipe).

Crème Fraîche

3 cups whipping cream

1 cup buttermilk

¼ cup fresh chives, finely chopped

Mix whipping cream and buttermilk and pour into a covered glass container. Leave at room temperature for 12 hours, then refrigerate for another 12 hours. The bottom of the container will be full of water. Scoop off the thick *crème fraîche*, which should be the consistency of sour cream. Fold in chives.

Oils and Reductions

Basil Oil

½ lb basil leaves

1 tsp salt

juice of 1 lemon

2 cups vegetable oil

Place basil leaves in boiling water for 10 seconds. Drain and quickly cool in cold water. Squeeze out all water and chop. Using a blender or food processor, purée with salt and lemon juice and vegetable oil. Blend on highest speed until warm, 10-15 minutes. Strain through a coffee filter.

Balsamic Reduction

4½ cups good quality balsamic vinegar

½ cup sugar

In a saucepan on medium heat, reduce by half. You can thicken by whisking in 2 tbsp cornstarch mixed with ¼ cup water.

Chile Oil

2 cups vegetable oil

¼ cup red chile flakes

¼ cup Spanish paprika

¼ cup Mexican chile powder

½ tsp salt

Whisk all ingredients together. In a medium-sized heavy-bottom pot on medium heat, cook mixture until chiles just start to brown. You do not want to burn them. Let cool to room temperature and strain through a coffee filter.

Lemon Curry Oil

2 cups vegetable oil

⅓ cup Madras curry powder

zest and juice of 2 lemons

½ tsp salt

Place all ingredients in a jar with a tight fitting lid. Shake until ingredients are well blended. Let sit 24 hours.

Roasting Garlic

Method 1: Drizzle whole heads with olive oil. Wrap in tin foil and bake in a 350°F oven until soft, about ½ hour. Let cool, and with a sharp serrated knife, cut off the root end of the garlic to expose the cloves. Squeeze the head of garlic to remove pulp. For a variation, drizzle with olive oil, season with a pinch of cracked chiles, a pinch of kosher salt, and fresh thyme.

Method 2: In a baking pan, combine 1 cup of peeled cloves and ¼ cup olive oil and roast in 350°F oven, tossing occasionally, until soft and golden, about 20 minutes.

Roasting Peppers

On grill: char peppers on all sides until black and blistered. Place in a bowl and cover with plastic wrap and let peppers steam.

In oven: toss the peppers in vegetable oil and place in pan on top rack of oven. Broil, turning frequently until the skin is blistered. Place in a bowl and cover with plastic wrap and let peppers steam.

Over gas: Place peppers directly over the flame and char evenly on all sides. Place in a bowl and cover with plastic wrap and let peppers steam.

For all methods: once peppers have cooled, peel away the charred skin and split open to remove stem and seeds.

Oven-Dried Tomatoes

Preheat oven to 150°F. Cut tomatoes in half and spread on a cookie sheet. Let dry in oven for 5 hours.

Handling Hot Peppers

The heat of peppers is concentrated in the seeds and veins. When seeding and handling hot peppers, wear kitchen or rubber gloves. After handling peppers, wash hands thoroughly in warm, soapy water. When using whole peppers in soups and stews, or puréeing them in food processors or blenders, the vapour coming off the peppers can be strong, so watch that you don't get the steam in your eyes.

Cooking Wild Rice

⅓ cup wild rice

2 cups of chicken stock

In a pot, simmer rice, covered for about 30-45 minutes, adding more stock, if necessary, until kernels are very soft and have popped. Drain and cool on a cookie sheet.

One-third cup of dry wild rice yields 1 cup of cooked rice.

Basic Stocks

Brown Veal Stock/Demi

Brown veal stock is used for sauces; white veal stock for soups.

4-5 lbs veal bones, cracked or cut in pieces by butcher

2 onions, quartered

2 carrots, quartered

2 stalks celery, cut into 2-inch pieces

1 clove garlic

12 cups water

1 tomato, chopped or 1 tsp tomato paste

1 large *bouquet garni* (green part of 1 leek, bay leaf, and fresh thyme)

10 peppercorns

Preheat oven to 450°F.

In a non-aluminum roasting pan, roast bones in oven until well browned, stirring occasionally, about 30-40 minutes. Add the vegetables and brown 15-20 minutes longer. Thorough browning gives stock flavour and colour.

Discard the fat from the pan and deglaze with 2 cups of the water. Add the remaining liquid, garlic, tomato, *bouquet garni*, and peppercorns.

(For additional colour, singe half an onion over an electric plate or gas burner and add to stock.)

Makes 2-3 quarts

White Veal Stock/Demi

Brown veal stock is used for sauces; white veal stock for soups.

4-5 lbs veal bones, cracked or cut in pieces by butcher

2 onions, quartered

2 carrots, quartered

2 stalks celery, cut into 2-inch pieces

1 clove garlic

12 cups water

1 large *bouquet garni* (green part of 1 leek, bay leaf, and fresh thyme)

10 peppercorns

Blanch the bones by bringing them to a boil in enough water to cover, then simmer 5 minutes. Drain and rinse.

In a non-aluminum stock pot, combine bones and vegetables. Add the garlic, water, *bouquet garni*, and peppercorns. Bring slowly to a boil, skimming often. Simmer for 4 to 5 hours, skimming occasionally. Stock should be reduced very slowly to avoid clouding.

Stain and taste the stock. If the flavour is not strong enough, boil until it is concentrated. Skim off any fat.

Chicken Stock

Substitute 3 lb chicken backs and necks, or whole fowl, for half the veal bones in the above recipe. Simmer stock for 3-4 hours. If using a fowl, remove it when thigh meat is tender and easily pierced with a skewer, about 1¼ to 1½ hours.

Makes 2-3 quarts

Halibut Stock/*Fumet*

1 tbsp butter

4 shallots, or 1 medium onion, finely chopped

1½ lb fish bones, cut up

1 cup white wine (or lemon juice)

water to cover

10 whole black peppercorns

1 large *bouquet garni* (green part of 1 leek, bay leaf, and fresh thyme)

2 celery stocks, chopped

3 garlic cloves

In a large non-aluminum stockpot, melt the butter and cook the onion slowly until it is soft but not brown. Add the fish bones, wine or lemon juice, water, peppercorns, and *bouquet garni*. Bring slowly to a boil, skimming often. Simmer, uncovered, for 20 minutes, then strain and leave to cool.

This recipe yields a neutral-flavoured fish stock. If you use wine instead of lemon juice, it is called a *fumet*.

Makes about 1 quart

Lobster/Shrimp Stock Infused with Saffron and Pernod

This stock is the base for lobster bisque or any rich seafood soup.

5 lbs lobster shells

5 lbs shrimp shells

1½ heads celery

5 large yellow onions

1 bulb garlic

5 heads fennel

2 large carrots

5 bay leaves

1 leek

6 tbsp olive oil

¼ lb butter

4 cups Pernod

1 cup white wine

6 tomatoes

2 grams saffron

Lobster and shrimp shells are readily available – and inexpensive – from your local fishmonger. Peel all vegetables and remove leaves from celery and tops from carrots. Dice all vegetables into 1½-inch pieces.

In a saucepan on medium heat, sauté the shells in olive oil until they are golden but not roasted. Reduce heat to medium and add butter.

When butter is melted, add vegetables except the tomatoes and cook over medium heat. Do not roast; just sweat.

Increase the heat and flambé with the Pernod and white wine. Add the tomatoes and saffron and enough water to barely cover. Bring to a boil, then simmer for 30 minutes, skimming constantly. Turn down heat. Cover pot with saran wrap for 5 minutes to allow the butter to rise to the surface. Skim butter. Pass stock through cheesecloth, then cool down.

Makes about 2-3 quarts

Bain-marie

A *bain-marie* is a water bath in which you place a container of food (pan, bowl, ramekin) in a large, shallow pan of warm water, which surrounds the food with gentle heat. The food may be cooked in this manner either in an oven or on top of a range. This technique is designed to cook delicate dishes such as custards, sauces, and savory mousses without breaking or curdling them.

Clarified Butter

Drawn butter is clarified butter. Take ½ lb butter and place in a pot on medium heat. With a ladle, skim off foam that rises to the surface. When butter is clear, add 4 sage leaves. Let stand on low heat until ready to serve.

Paneer

Paneer is an East Indian yogurt cheese. To make: place organic plain yogurt in a coffee filter-lined, or cheesecloth-lined colander. Place a bowl underneath colander. Cover yogurt with plastic wrap. Put in fridge for 24 hours until all liquid has drained from the yogurt. About 2 cups of yogurt yields the 1 cup required in the recipes.

Master Pizza Dough

1 7-gram pkg active dry yeast

1½ cups all-purpose flour

1½ cups cake flour

1 tsp salt

extra-virgin olive oil

½ cup cornmeal

In a large mixing bowl, dissolve yeast in ¼ cup lukewarm water. Set aside until yeast begins to activate (it will foam a little), about 10 minutes.

In a separate mixing bowl, combine flours and salt. Add one cup of flour mixture to yeast mixture and stir well. The dough should be soft but not too wet.

Turn dough out on a lightly floured surface and knead with the heels of your palms until dough has a smooth, uniform texture, about 10-12 minutes. Divide dough into 2 even-sized balls.

Coat the insides of 2 medium bowls with ½ tsp olive oil each. Place dough in bowls, cover with damp cloths or plastic wrap, and set aside to rise until double in bulk, about 2½-3 hours.

Place a pizza stone, or unglazed tile, in oven and preheat at highest setting before broil.

Sprinkle a baking sheet with cornmeal. Punch down dough from 1 bowl, make a ball and flatten it on the pan, taking care not to overwork the dough, stretch it into a thin, 12-inch circle with a slightly raised edge.

Add topping and slide onto hot pizza stone.

Bake until crust is golden brown and crisp, about 12-15 minutes.

Meanwhile, prepare second pizza. Remove first from oven and bake the second on the same stone.

Drizzle a little olive oil on each before serving.

Variation: Navajo Fry Bread
  Roll dough into 3-inch balls. Coat lightly with cornmeal. Roll or pat flat, cut into squares, and deep-fry at 360°F until bread floats and is golden and lightly crisped.

Peeling and Deveining Shrimp

Using your hands, peel shells starting the underside, along the feelers. If the intestinal vein that runs along the back is visible (black), remove it with the tip of a sharp paring knife.

Cleaning Mussels

Rinse mussels in the sink with running water continuously to remove exterior sand and dirt.

Cleaning Squid

Using a sharp knife, cut off the head, tentacles, and the fin. Pull out the clear, plastic-looking blade that runs the length of the body. Pull out the rest of the innards. Rinse tentacles, mantle (body cavity), and fins in clean water. Be sure the body cavity is clean of all body fluids, membranes, and innards.

Home Smoking

The idea behind smoking is to impart the flavour of what you are using as a smoking object into the ingredients. If the ingredients become too dry, reconstitute the item in liquid to make them supple and palatable.

Start with a large metal pan, with similarly fitting perforated pan. These are known as hotel pans and can be sourced from your local restaurant supplier. (The other option is to use a wok with a cookie-cooling tray placed in the centre.) Generally, it is recommended to use a mixture of sugar and salt in equal proportions with enough water to cover the item that will be smoked. This is called a brine, an important procedure for seafood and some meats.

Preheat oven to between 150 and 400°F. 150° is considered a cold smoke and 400° is a hot smoke. Essentially, the difference between a cold and a hot smoke is that a hot smoke is fully cooked, whereas a cold smoke is only scented with the smoke or, in other words, cured.

Cover either the pan or the wok with tinfoil. Place your smoking items on the tinfoil. Depending on the flavour you wish to impart to the food, be creative. Think of things that might smoke – aromas you enjoy – like tea leaves, chile peppers, bay leaves, lemongrass, and of course, apple wood, cherry wood, or alder wood.

Suggested smoking times:

Chicken and lamb: smoke through until cooked, about 20-30 minutes.

Tomatoes: about 10 minutes. Leave to cool, covered, in pan.

Fish: about 10-15 minutes, depending on thickness.

Cocktail Party

Smoky Orange Chile and
Thai Basil Sauce Mussels

My burnt-orange chipotle sauce only has 2 ingredients. The key is incorporating the chipotle when the juice has reached the bitter-orange stage so that the flavour changes from sweet to savory. I am presenting the sauce here with P.E.I. mussels from Canada's east coast. They tend to be very plump with a pleasant salty-sweet brine. The sauce doesn't require any meat stock, so it can be readily adapted for vegetarians. Leftover sauce can be refrigerated for up to 1 month, or frozen for 6.

3 cups frozen orange juice concentrate

2 tbsp chipotle peppers, puréed

2 tbsp good quality olive oil

2 cloves garlic, finely chopped

1 shallot, finely chopped

pinch red chile flakes

5 sprigs fresh Thai basil

1 lb fresh P.E.I. mussels, bearded and rinsed (see page 23)

¼ cup dry white wine

2 tbsp unsalted butter

If you add ½ cup whipping cream to the sauce, just after you add the wine and orange juice, you have classic Maltaise sauce, which is an orange-scented Hollandaise. Unlike the regular sauce, this variation must be used the same day.

In a saucepan on medium heat, cook orange juice until it is caramelized and rust-coloured. Taste it too: the juice should be slightly tart. At this point, add the chipotle pepper, turn heat down to low, and simmer for 10 minutes.

In a large frying pan or medium saucepan on high heat, lightly sauté the garlic and shallot with the chile flakes. Stir in mussels quickly. Add white wine and orange juice.

Cover and allow mussels to steam for 2 minutes. Remove lid, add basil and butter. Stir and cover for another 2 minutes. Discard any unopened mussels.

Serves 4

Beverage Pairing: Voignier or Belgium-style golden ale

3-Chile Marinated Sweet Potato-Wrapped Prawns with Lip-Smacking Tomato and Sweet Chile Dipping Sauce

This recipe was developed for a party I have every year called the "Bindustry Party" where I invite chefs, servers, hotel concierges, and others in the food, beverage, and hospitality industry to have a night off and celebrate food and the industry we all work hard in. Because these people make up a good percentage of my clientele, it is also my opportunity to show my appreciation to them.

These prawns are fast and easy to make and they rock, kind of like my party guests. And wait till ya see what the yam wrap looks like coming out of the fryer: it's kinda reminiscent of your after-midnight hair "do's" and "don't's."

Sweet Potato-Wrapped Prawns

¼ cup chile oil (see page 14)

2 tbsp puréed chipotle pepper

1 tbsp red chile flakes

1 bunch fresh cilantro, chopped

1 tbsp puréed garlic

1 tbsp hoi sin sauce

1 tsp sea salt

1 lb large tiger prawns, peeled and deveined (see page 23)

2 large sweet potatoes or yams, peeled

vegetable oil for deep-frying

In a large bowl, combine all ingredients except potatoes. Marinate, covered, in the fridge for 4-5 hours.

Using a mandoline or a food processor fitted with a julienne cutting blade, cut sweet potatoes into spaghetti-like strands.

Remove prawns from marinade and wrap 6 or 7 sweet potato strands around each one. (They should adhere easily to the marinade.)

In a deep-fat fryer at 360°F start deep-frying prawns in small batches of 7 to 10 for approximately 2 minutes. Prawns will float to the surface when ready. The sweet potato strands should be crispy and golden brown.

Lip-Smacking Tomato and Sweet Chile Dipping Sauce

2 large ripe flavourful tomatoes
½ bunch fresh cilantro
½ red onion
2-3 tbsp Asian sweet chile sauce
1 large clove garlic, peeled
salt and pepper to taste

In a food processor, purée all ingredients. Strain.
Yields about 1½ cups and should be used the same day.

To Plate: Self-serve platter style. Dip in! Fill your boots!

Serves 4

Beverage Pairing: Off-dry German Riesling (Kabinett)

Scallop and Tiger Prawn Tournedos with Bonito Butter Sauce, Leek Tempura, and Cucumber Salsa

This recipe produces 1 exact portion of how we serve it (2 skewers each), so each person gets 4 prawns and 2 scallops (I use Digby Bay scallops from the east coast). Simply multiply the recipe ingredients by the number of guests you have. The salsa is best served the day it is made. The vegetables should be diced as finely as possible, a culinary term the French call *brunoise*. It's a great side dish with the tornedos, but is good served with any grilled fish.

Scallop and Tiger Prawn Tournedos with Bonito Butter Sauce

4 large tiger prawns

2 large scallops

1 oven-dried Roma tomato (see page 16)

salt and freshly cracked black pepper to taste

2 oz white wine

½ tsp bonito flakes

1 tbsp unsalted butter

2 6-inch bamboo skewers, soaked overnight in water

Preheat oven to 400°F.

Alternating prawn/scallop/prawn, thread seafood onto 2 bamboo skewers ending with 2 prawns and 1 scallop.

In an ovenproof skillet on high, cook tomatoes in olive oil until juice begins to release in the oil, about 1 minute.

Place skewers of prawns and scallops in the pan and sear for 1 minute on each side. Season with salt and pepper.

Flip skewers over, place pan in oven for 3 minutes. Remove prawns and scallops from pan and set aside. Do not remove tomatoes; they will keep adding flavour to the sauce.

On high heat, deglaze the pan with white wine. Add bonito flakes and reduce until there is almost no liquid left. Remove pan from heat. Stir in butter to emulsify. Garnish skewers with tobiko and sesame seeds if desired before serving.

Leek Tempura

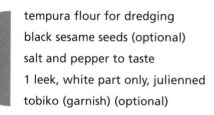

tempura flour for dredging

black sesame seeds (optional)

salt and pepper to taste

1 leek, white part only, julienned

tobiko (garnish) (optional)

In a medium-sized bowl, combine flour, salt, and pepper. Lightly toss leek in flour mixture, shaking off any excess flour before cooking in a deep-fat fryer at 360°F. Test by dropping in 1 leek strip: it should float to the top and bubble rapidly. Do not burn leek strips or they will be bitter. Garnish with a good pinch of tobiko just before serving.

Cucumber Salsa

1 long English cucumber, finely diced

1 large red pepper, finely diced

1 medium red onion, finely diced

1 oz apple cider vinegar

1 oz mirin

juice of 1 lemon

2 tbsp Thai basil, or cilantro

1 tsp salt

1 pinch red chile flakes

dash hot sauce

Combine all ingredients.

To Plate: Arrange skewers on top of each other, or standing up. Pour sauce over scallops and rest crispy leek tempura atop scallops. Place tomato halves from sauce on either side and add a tsp of cucumber salsa on top of each half.

Serves 4

Beverage Pairing: **Full-bodied Pinôt Blanc**

Scallop Ceviche with Minted Watermelon and Coconut Foam

Ceviche is a fast and healthy way to enjoy fresh seafood. A staple of Latin American diets, I guess you could say it's the Latin version of sushi.

The acid from the lemon and lime actually cooks the fish. When you see it turn from translucent to opaque, you know it's ready. You can ceviche prawns, squid, octopus, and lobster. Ah, what the heck! Run the gamut! Go nuts! Be creative!

12 large scallops, rinsed and dried

3 lemons

5 limes

1 tsp sea salt

1 Thai bird chile, diced

1 small watermelon, seeds removed, cut into 1-inch cubes

1 bunch fresh mint, chopped

⅛ cup mirin

⅛ cup rice wine vinegar

1 12-oz can coconut milk

1 one-inch piece fresh ginger, finely grated

½ tsp togarashi (garnish)

Slice each scallop into 3 even discs. Place in bowl. Add juice from the 3 lemons and 3 of the 5 limes. Season with sea salt and add Thai chile. Marinate 15 minutes to ½ hour.

In a separate bowl, combine watermelon cubes with chopped mint, mirin, and rice wine vinegar. Marinate for 15 minutes to ½ hour.

In a third bowl, combine juice of the 2 remaining limes with coconut milk and ginger. Using your blender or the steam attachment on your espresso machine, foam the milk.

To Plate: Spray coconut foam onto platter. Arrange marinated scallops and minted watermelon beside foam. Dust with togarashi.

Serves 4

Beverage Pairing: Carib Lager

Salmon and Tuna Tartare

8 oz fresh wild sockeye salmon, finely cubed

8 oz Ahi or Albacore tuna, finely cubed

For Tuna Tartare Marinade:

½ Asian pear, finely cubed

juice of 1 lime

3 tbsp soda water

1 tsp oyster sauce

1 tbsp sweet chile

⅛ cup sesame oil

juice of 2 lemons

juice of 2 oranges

1 tsp kecap manis

1 tsp mirin

Mix cubed pear and combine with lime juice and soda water.

Combine with remaining marinade ingredients and marinate tuna
for ½ hour.

For Salmon Tartare Marinade:

¼ tsp togarashi

⅛ tsp Worcestershire sauce

⅛ tsp tahini

¼ cup Roast Garlic Miso Aioli (see page 50)

⅛ cup extra-virgin olive oil

1 shallot, minced

1 tbsp capers, minced

Combine all ingredients for marinade.

To Plate: Using a ring mould, assemble salmon on bottom, tuna and pear mixture on top. Remove mould from ingredients, which should stand up intact.

Serves 4

Beverage Pairing: **Malvasia or Albarino**

Cold-Smoked Halibut Brandade

"Gordo's" West Coast version of salt cod or *bacalao brandade*, a staple in Spain and Portugal. Designed before refrigeration, salted cod could be preserved and kept indefinitely, then reconstituted with a liquid to make it palatable. This version is a modern adaptation that keeps nicely in the fridge for up to 7 days. Serve it to thoroughly modern Millie. Hey, Millie! She likes it!

½ cup sugar

½ cup sea salt

4 cups water

3 lbs halibut fillets

2 smoking chips, broken up (see page 24)

¼ cup capers

juice of 2 lemons

1 dash Tabasco sauce

½ cup Spanish extra-virgin olive oil

salt and white pepper to taste

To smoke, take a large pan lined with foil, add smoking chips and place over burner. Place halibut in a perforated tray over chips and cover with aluminum foil. Let smoke for about 5 minutes on BBQ or on medium-high heat on a stovetop grill.

To make halibut brandade, begin by dissolving sugar and salt in water to create a brine. Soak halibut in brine for at least 4 hours. Drain and smoke for 5 minutes (see sidebar).

In the meantime, preheat oven to 400°F.

When the halibut has finished smoking, transfer smoking unit to the oven until halibut is cooked but retains juice, about 10 minutes. Let cool.

When cooled, place halibut in a food processor along with the capers, lemon juice, and Tabasco sauce. Add olive oil and pulse until puréed. Season with salt and white pepper to taste. The purée should be creamy, so you may need to add a bit more olive oil to achieve this consistency.

To Plate: Serve with lemon curry oil (see page 14).

Serves 4

Beverage Pairing: California Chardonnay

Ancho Chile-Dusted and Fragrant Lime Beef Tenderloin Pickup Sticks

Bold flavours and melt-in-your-mouth texture. A simple "wow" item for any cocktail party, or any day of the week, for that matter. They're wonderful on the BBQ or done under the broiler. Good served with shitake mushrooms or sweet, in-season tomatoes.

½ cup ancho chile pepper, toasted

½ tsp cayenne pepper

1 tsp sea salt

3 lbs Angus or other good quality beef tenderloin

For Marinade:

2 small cans frozen Filipino lime juice

½ cup garlic, chopped

2 cups banana ketchup

½ cup soy sauce

¼ cup sambel olek

½ cup canola oil

seeds from 2 pomegranates (garnish)

24 wooden skewers, soaked in water overnight

To make chile mixture, toast ancho chile pepper in a 350°F oven until supple and aromatic, about 7 minutes. Let cool, then grind until powdered or flaky. Combine with cayenne pepper and sea salt.

Cut beef tenderloin against the grain into 1-inch cubes. In a large bowl, mix all marinade ingredients. Add cubed beef and mix with your hands until beef is well coated. Cover and let marinate overnight in the fridge.

The next day, skewer each stick with about 3 oz meat. Grill on BBQ or broil in the oven, 3½ minutes each side for medium-rare.

To Plate: **Place on platter. Sprinkle pomegranate seeds on top.**

Serves 12

Beverage Pairing: **Sangiovese**

Crispy Risotto Balls with Gooey Cheese Centres

1 yellow onion, diced

2 tbsp olive oil

3 tbsp butter

3 cups arborio rice

1 cup white wine

2 sprigs fresh thyme

2 bay leaves

6 litres chicken stock (see page 18)

3 tbsp butter

¾ cup Parmesan cheese, freshly grated

1 lb gouda cheese, cubed

panko flakes for coating

vegetable oil for deep-frying

In a wide and deep heavy-bottomed pan, sweat onion in olive oil and butter. Add rice and toss to coat. Deglaze with white wine, thyme, and bay leaves.

When all the wine has been absorbed, add chicken broth, 1 ladle (about 5 oz or just enough to cover all the rice) at a time, stirring constantly until risotto is fully cooked and all the liquid has been absorbed. Add butter, Parmesan cheese, and stir to incorporate. Remove and spread on a tray to cool.

When rice has cooled, form into 2 oz balls and stuff a piece of diced gouda in the centre. Roll in panko flakes.

Heat oil in deep-fat fryer to 350°F. Drop in risotto balls and cook until golden brown.

Serves 4

Beverage Pairing: **Merlot**

Oven-Dried Tomato and Goat Cheese Salsa

A crowd pleaser extraordinaire. By unlocking the Timothy Leary portion of my cranium, I was able to come up with this highly addictive salsa. It should be dark red with bits of white, not a rosé colour.

The salsa lasts 5 days in the fridge. You can make the tomato purée up to 1 month ahead, freeze it, and add goat cheese and fresh basil just before serving.

12 oven-dried Roma tomatoes (see page 16)

⅓ cup goat cheese

20 leaves fresh basil

2 tbsp chipotle peppers

salt and pepper to taste

In a food processor, pulse tomatoes, goat cheese, basil, chipotle peppers, salt, and pepper to make a chunky salsa.

Yields 2 cups

Beverage Pairing: **Micro-brewed pale ale**

Gorgonzola Bruschetta

This recipe uses a traditional pesto so it can be mixed with a splash of dry white wine and a touch of whipping cream and used on linguine. For a non-traditional pesto, substitute ½ cup fresh cilantro for basil and ⅓ cup toasted almonds, skins on, for the pine nuts.

2 cloves garlic

1 oz extra-virgin olive oil

⅛ cup pine nuts

juice of 1 lemon

⅛ cup Parmesan cheese, freshly grated

1 cup fresh basil, without stems

1 tsp cracked black pepper

salt to taste

2 pieces focaccia bread, lightly oiled and grilled

3 oz Gorgonzola cheese

In a food processor, purée garlic, olive oil, and pine nuts until smooth. Add remaining ingredients and purée until pesto is a smooth, paste-like consistency. Correct flavours you want to be prominent, like basil or Parmesan.

Spread pesto on the grilled focaccia. Place Gorgonzola in little chunks on top. Broil in oven until the cheese melts. Garnish with a sprinkling of grated Parmesan cheese or balsamic reduction and oven-dried tomatoes (see page 16).

Serves 4

Sevruga Caviar and *Crème Fraîche*-Stuffed New Crop or Nugget Potatoes

What can I say? Three great flavours that simply work together: a clean, mean, tapas machine. Minimalist in preparation and architecturally beautiful in appearance. If this were a sofa, it would be from the Bauhaus School of Design.

12 small red or white nugget potatoes, washed

2 oz unsalted butter

1 tsp salt

1 tsp cracked black pepper

1 cup *crème fraîche* (see page 12)

1 1-oz tin of good quality Russian sevruga caviar

Preheat oven to 400°F.

In an ovenproof skillet, toss potatoes with butter, salt, and pepper and lightly sauté until skins start to brown. Place skillet in oven until skins start to wrinkle and potatoes feel soft, about 20-30 minutes.

To Plate: Using a sharp knife, cut a cross in top of potatoes and lightly squeeze bottom sides to force top open. Place a small dollop of *crème fraîche* and caviar on top of each potato. Serve hot.

Serves 4

Beverage Pairing: Sancerre

Dense Belgian Chocolate Warm Brownie Cakes

6 oz dark chocolate

2 oz whipping cream

4 oz roasted hazelnut paste

3 large eggs

¼ cup white sugar

Kahlua

whipping cream

seasonal berries

icing sugar

crème Anglais (see page 12)

Hazelnut Paste

To make hazelnut paste, roast hazelnuts in a 375°F oven until brown, about 10 minutes, then purée in a food processor.

Preheat oven to 350°F.

In a double boiler, melt chocolate with cream and hazelnut paste. Set aside but keep warm.

In a separate double boiler, whip eggs and sugar until warm and frothy, being careful not to scramble the eggs. Fold in chocolate and egg mixture.

Fill 4 to 6 lightly greased ramekins ¾ full with mixture. Place ramekins on a tray and bake in oven for 15 minutes.

To Plate: Slice cakes in half. Pour slightly warmed Kahlua onto cut portions. Fill bottom half with freshly whipped cream and fresh seasonal berries. Put top back on, dust with icing sugar and pool *crème Anglais* around cake.

Serves 4

Beverage Pairing: **Framboise**

BBQ

Grilled Asparagus

2 lbs fresh asparagus

2 oz extra-virgin olive oil

salt and pepper

juice of 1 lemon

1 cup asiago cheese, shaved

Try to pick thin asparagus stems, or peel thin stems. Bend the asparagus and let them break to find the natural tender point. Discard the bottom ends and cut each end neatly on the bias. Brush with olive oil, season with salt and pepper. Grill until tender, turning once after 5 minutes.

To Plate: Arrange neatly on a serving platter and drizzle with extra-virgin olive oil and fresh lemon juice. Sprinkle with shaved asiago.

Serves 4

Beverage Pairing: New Zealand Sauvignon Blanc

BBQ Portobello Mushroom Cutlet and Seasonal Vegetables with Roast Garlic Balsamic Jam

The quintessential vegetarian equivalent to steak. Even the pet rabbit won't go hungry at your backyard shindig.

BBQ Portobello Mushroom Cutlet and Seasonal Vegetables

½ lb new crop nugget potatoes, blanched

¼ cup butter

salt and pepper to taste

1 sprig of fresh rosemary

1 bunch each baby carrots/baby zucchini/ baby squash/French beans/ trimmed asparagus

½ red bell pepper

2 bunches baby bok choy

1 tbsp zatar

zest and juice of 1 lemon

salt and pepper to taste

⅛ cup extra-virgin olive oil

4 large portobello mushrooms, stems removed

salt and pepper to taste

2 tbsp balsamic vinegar

Preheat oven or grill to 400°F.

Wrap blanched potatoes in tin foil with ¼ cup butter, salt, pepper, and fresh rosemary. Roast or grill, turning package regularly, until potatoes are tender, about 20 minutes.

In a bowl, toss trimmed vegetables with zatar, lemon, salt, pepper, and olive oil. Let stand 10 minutes before grilling.

On a baking sheet, lay portobello caps sides up. Sprinkle with salt, pepper, olive oil, and balsamic vinegar. Roast or grill for 10 minutes each side. Remove and let cool.

Roast or grill vegetables approximately 7 minutes, before potatoes are ready.

Roast Garlic Balsamic Jam

1 tbsp cornstarch

¼ cup balsamic vinegar

¼ cup sugar

3 cups balsamic vinegar

1 tbsp unsalted butter

4 to 5 large cloves roasted garlic (see page 15)

In a small bowl, dissolve cornstarch in ¼ cup balsamic vinegar. Whisk in sugar.

In a small saucepan (preferably non-reactive stainless steel), on medium heat, reduce remaining balsamic vinegar by ½. Add cornstarch and sugar mixture and cook, whisking continuously, until jam is slightly thickened, about 3 to 5 minutes. To finish, stir in butter and roasted garlic.

To Plate: Create a stack of equal amounts of vegetables and potatoes in middle of plate. Place mushroom on top of stack. Dress with warm roast garlic balsamic jam.

Serves 4

Beverage Pairing: **Ripasso Valpolicella**

BBQ Oysters in Shell with Snake Bite Salsa and Sangrita

This recipe uses as many oysters as you can eat and also works for clams and mussels.

Shuck the oysters, but don't tip out the juice or rinse under water to remove shell fragments. BBQ in half-shell or whole. The oysters will open when done. You can also BBQ them naked – the oysters, that is – just until they are warm in the middle and a touch crispy on the outside. Remember: find the art!

Snake Bite Salsa

4 vine-ripened tomatoes, *concassé*

1 sprig tarragon, chopped

¼ cup lager beer

⅛ cup apple cider

1 jalapeño pepper, seeded and chopped (see page 16)

salt and pepper to taste

A traditional Mexican accompaniment to tequila, Sangrita is meant to be served with authentic Blue Agave. This recipe yields about 1 cup and will last for 5 days in the refrigerator. In addition to being a sauce for BBQ oysters, try a dash in a martini or in a ceviche of prawns or fish. Up the ante with a splash of tequila.

To *concassé* tomatoes, take a sharp knife and make an X in the top. Plunge into boiling water for 20 seconds. Remove, and place immediately in ice water to stop cooking. Skin will lift at the corners of the X. Peel skin and squeeze out seeds. Chop coarsely.

In a large bowl, mix tomatoes with remaining ingredients. Let stand 1 hour at room temperature before serving.

Sangrita

12 ripe Roma, or heirloom variety, tomatoes

juice of 1 lemon

juice of 1 lime

juice of 1 orange

½ tsp salt

½ tsp ground white pepper

dash Tabasco or favourite hot sauce

In a food processor or blender, purée all ingredients together and strain.
  Place in a sealed container.

Serves 4

Beverage Pairing: Lager, Tequila, or Vodka

Whole BBQ Trout with Aromatics and Toasted Almond and Basmati Rice Pilaf

Out of the frying pan and into the fire! Take this recipe with you on the fishing trip to your favourite lake. Don't forget the waterproof matches. I like using Meyer lemons in this recipe, but any kind will do.

4 1-lb fresh lake, golden or rainbow trout

sea salt and freshly ground black pepper to taste

½ cup basmati rice, toasted and ground

4 large fennel tops or fronds

4 lemons, thinly sliced

4 sprigs fresh thyme

½ cup sage-drawn butter (see page 21)

juice of 1 lemon

Clean fish. Rub cavity with a mixture of the sea salt, pepper, and toasted basmati. Fill cavities with fennel tops, sliced lemon, and thyme. Tie closed, if necessary.

BBQ for about 5 minutes on each side. Fish should be moist and juicy. Remove aromatics before serving.

Toasted Almond and Basmati Rice Pilaf

2 cups basmati rice, rinsed

½ white onion, diced

3 cups chicken stock (see page 18) or water with 3 bay leaves

¼ cup butter

In a saucepan with a lid, on medium heat, sauté onion in butter until translucent. Add rice and stir to coat. Salt and pepper to taste. Add stock and bring to a boil. Cover tightly and cook on low heat for 15-20 minutes.

Turn off heat, but do not lift lid! Let stand 15 minutes.

To Plate: Dress plated whole fish with sage-drawn butter and freshly squeezed lemon juice. Serve with rice pilaf.

Serves 4

Beverage Pairing: BC Pinôt Gris

Bonfire-Style Wild Sockeye Salmon, Roast Garlic Miso Aioli, and Wild Rice Waldorf Salad

The rich, oily salmon flavour really comes through with this simple approach especially when paired with this modern, healthy adaptation of the classic Waldorf Salad.

Bonfire-Style Wild Sockeye Salmon

8 sprigs each of fresh rosemary, thyme, oregano

4 tbsp olive oil

salt and white pepper to taste

4 6-oz fresh wild sockeye salmon fillets

Let herbs dry overnight on a paper towel in a warm place.

Oil each fillet and season with salt and pepper. Press herbs on top of fillets and place on a hot grill. Press inverted pan over salmon so that herbs will smoke and smolder. Cook salmon on one side only until rare or medium-rare, about 10 minutes.

Remove from grill, trying to leave the herbs attached.

Roast Garlic Miso Aioli

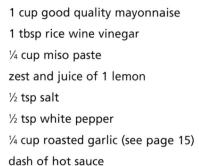

1 cup good quality mayonnaise

1 tbsp rice wine vinegar

¼ cup miso paste

zest and juice of 1 lemon

½ tsp salt

½ tsp white pepper

¼ cup roasted garlic (see page 15)

dash of hot sauce

In a food processor, blend all ingredients until smooth.

Wild Rice Waldorf Salad

4 large Granny Smith apples, thinly sliced

1 oz lemon juice

2 cups celery root, julienned

1 oz lemon juice (for celery)

¼ cup walnut pieces

¼ bunch of fresh flat leaf (Italian) parsley leaves

Toss apple slices in lemon juice. In a separate bowl, toss celery root with lemon juice.

Combine all salad ingredients in a serving bowl and toss with aioli.

To Plate: Divide salad onto 4 serving plates and place salmon fillets on top. Garnish with a drizzle of fresh lemon juice, extra-virgin olive oil, and extra aioli. Serve with cooked wild rice (see page 16).

Beverage Pairing: **Oregon Style Light Pinôt Noir**

BBQ Chicken in a Roast Garlic Crust Served with Romesco Sauce

2 cups olive oil

zest of 1 orange

2 tbsp capers, chopped

1 tbsp cumin seeds, toasted

1 tsp sea salt

1 tbsp freshly ground black pepper

1 bay leaf

4 sprigs fresh rosemary, chopped

8 pieces chicken breasts and thighs

In a large bowl, combine ingredients and marinate chicken, covered, in the fridge for 24 hours.

For Crust:

12 cloves roasted garlic (see page 15)

½ cup butter-roasted croutons

½ tsp sea salt

1 tsp freshly ground black pepper

1 tbsp olive oil

In a food processor, purée all ingredients to form a paste. Set aside.

Grill chicken until juice runs clear when thickest part is poked and the meat isn't pink inside. Crust skin side of chicken with garlic paste. Cook a further 5 minutes with the lid down. Crust will adhere and be slightly crispy. In fact, chicken needs to be charred somewhat to achieve a smoky flavour. It should never come off the grill anemic-looking.

Romesco Sauce

You can freeze this sauce or keep it in a covered container for up to 1 week in refrigerator. Also makes an excellent sauce for mussels.

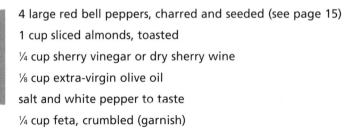

4 large red bell peppers, charred and seeded (see page 15)

1 cup sliced almonds, toasted

¼ cup sherry vinegar or dry sherry wine

⅛ cup extra-virgin olive oil

salt and white pepper to taste

¼ cup feta, crumbled (garnish)

In a food processor or blender, purée all ingredients, except feta, until smooth.

In a saucepan on medium, heat sauce. Add the feta.

To Plate: Pool sauce in centre of platter and arrange chicken neatly in middle, stacking high so sauce is exposed on the sides. For extra kick, drizzle with chile oil (see page 14).

Serves 4

Beverage Pairing: **Medium-bodied Chianti**

Tandoori Lamb Ribs and Potato Paratha with Grapefruit-Scented Paneer

This might seem like a big recipe. However, when you wrap your gums around these puppies, you won't find yourself asking, "Where's the beef?"

BBQs have a way of turning into large backyard parties, so it's good to have a recipe that can accommodate them, and here it is: my version of a lamb curry. I love lamb but I also love ribs, so I blended the two to come up with this "best of both worlds" recipe.

And here's the best part: once the ribs are braised, they will keep in the braising liquid for 5 days in the fridge, so you don't have to chow them all down in one sitting.

Brine for 8 large racks of lamb ribs:

4½ cups beer

4½ cups water

1 cup sugar

1 cup salt

Mix well before adding to lamb. Smoke lamb (see page 24).

For Braising:

4½ cups beer

4½ cups veal stock (see page 17) and water to cover lamb, if necessary

6 bay leaves

4 tomatoes, chopped

1 onion, chopped

¼ cup whole coriander seeds

¼ cup whole cardamom seeds

1 small piece of ginger

⅛ cup chile flakes

salt and pepper to taste

honey to taste

1 12-oz jar tandoori paste

½ 12-oz jar tamarind paste

Preheat oven to 350°F.

Place smoked lamb in a large roasting pan with all of
the braising ingredients.

Cover pan with foil or lid and braise in the oven until meat is almost falling
off the bone, about 1½ hours. Set aside to cool. Strain braising liquid. Grill
lamb 1 minute each side, using the reserved liquid as a glaze.

Potato Paratha

For Dough:

3 cups flour

1 tsp salt

1 cup water

¼ cup vegetable oil

In a large mixing bowl, combine flour and salt. Add water and vegetable oil
and mix to form dough. Do not knead. Form into 2-3-inch balls and let
rest about 15 minutes.

For Filling:

2 large onions, diced

3 tbsp clarified butter (see page 21)

8 cardamom seeds

2 tbsp fenugreek

2 tbsp coriander seeds

3 tbsp garam masala

2 tbsp cumin seeds

2 tbsp fennel seeds

3 whole allspice berries, ground

6 cloves

2 medium yams, boiled and peeled

10 purple potatoes, boiled and peeled

12 russet potatoes, boiled and peeled

6 tsp asafetida powder

2 tbsp black onion seeds

3 cups fresh snap peas, blanched and chopped

2-3 tbsp honey (optional)

In a saucepan on medium heat, sweat onions in clarified butter.

In a hot frying pan, toast all spices except black onion seeds and asafetida. Combine spices with onion and incorporate cooked yams and potatoes in a separate pot. Add asafetida, black onion seeds, and snap peas to potato filling. Taste and add honey if you think the mixture is too bitter. Set aside to cool.

Preheat oven to 375°F.

Roll out the dough balls into circles. Fill each with 2-3 tbsp of filling and fold over to form a half-moon. Crimp the sides, pinching tightly to seal.

In a deep-fat fryer at 350°F, gently lower each paratha and fry until light golden brown. Finish in the oven until fully golden brown and warm inside.

Grapefruit Scented Paneer

1 cup paneer (see page 21)

1 vanilla bean

1 pink grapefruit

2 sprigs fresh mint leaves, chopped

Slice vanilla bean lengthwise, scrape out seeds, and combine with paneer. Cut skin off grapefruit and flay (cut segments from the pith). Roughly chop grapefruit and combine with the vanilla paneer. Squeeze the leftover pith to get all remaining juice. Add chopped mint. Let stand 24 hours in refrigerator.

To Plate: Serve ribs and paratha on separate platters, with paneer on the side. Let guests help themselves.

Serves 4

Beverage Pairing: **Riesling or Voignier**

Buffalo Loin, Goat Cheese, and Shitake Mushroom Grilled Pizza

BBQ pizza is a nice alternative to oven-baked pizza and works well for an outdoor summer party. You can make individual pizzas or a single large one. The grill will impart a smoky flavour to the crust and topping and you can throw dried herbs or wood chips onto the flames to give the pizzas extra pizzazz. For a crisper, flatter crust, don't let the dough rise after rolling into pizza shape. For a thicker crust, let rise 10-15 minutes.

1 lb buffalo loin

salt and pepper to taste

1 lb shitake mushrooms, halved

¼ lb butter

½ bunch cilantro

½ bunch rosemary

pinch red chile flakes

1 Master Pizza Dough (see page 22)

cornmeal for dusting

⅛ cup olive oil

1 small jar hoi sin sauce

1 cup yellow cherry tomatoes, halved

½ lb goat cheese

Slice buffalo loin into ⅓-inch thick slices and rub lightly with olive oil. Season with salt and pepper and sear lightly on the grill for about 30 seconds each side. Set aside.

In a skillet on hot heat, sauté mushrooms in butter until softened. Season with salt and pepper. Add cilantro, rosemary, and chile flakes and set aside.

Roll pizza dough as thinly as possible into 6-inch rounds. Coat bottoms with cornmeal to add crunch and to keep dough from sticking to the grill. Brush tops with olive oil. With the back of a spoon, smear heaping tbsp of hoi sin sauce on top then arrange buffalo slices, mushrooms, and cherry tomatoes on top. Dot with medium-sized chunks of goat cheese.

Place on grill and close lid. Cook for 5-7 minutes, spinning pizzas occasionally to avoid burning.

Serves 4

Beverage Pairing: Lighter Côte de Rhone/Vaqueyras

New York Steak with Horseradish Asiago Crust, Campfire Hash

At the Bins we use a cut called "Newport," which is a hybrid of New York and top sirloin steak, and is cut specially for us.

New York Steak with Horseradish Asiago Crust

1 6-inch horseradish root or ¼ cup processed horseradish

1 tsp butter

½ cup butter

4 4-oz New York steaks

⅛ cup olive oil

salt and pepper to taste

½ cup medium asiago cheese, grated

Using a fine grater or rasp, grate horseradish if using root. Sweat in 1 tsp butter. Set aside.

In a food processor, whip ½ cup butter. Add to horseradish. Using saran wrap, roll mixture into a small log. Refrigerate until set.

Season steaks with olive oil, salt, and pepper. Grill for 2½ minutes each side for a rare steak. Remove from heat. Slice a puck of butter from roll and put on top of steak. Add 1 tbsp Asiago cheese and put into oven on broil just long enough to melt cheese and butter.

Campfire Hash

½ cup Pancetta, thinly sliced, diced

½ cup double-smoked bacon, thinly sliced, diced

2 tbsp butter

2 large russet potatoes, cubed into 1-inch pieces and blanched

1 large yam, cubed into 1-inch pieces and blanched

1 large celery root, cubed into 1-inch pieces and blanched

2 medium parsnips, cubed into 1-inch pieces and blanched

½ cup finely chopped flat leaf (Italian) parsley

While the steaks are on the grill, combine bacon and pancetta in a frying pan in butter on medium heat. Add blanched vegetables and sauté. Finish in the oven to warm throughout. Season to taste. Before serving, mix in parsley.

To Plate: Put vegetables in ring moulds. Set steak on top. Finish with a bit of demi-glace (see page 17), and mount with the rest of the horseradish butter.

Serves 4

Beverage Pairing: Australian Shiraz

Wild Sockeye Salmon in Cedar Sheath and Cedar Gelée Glazed Baby Vegetables with Apricot Fig Riesling Nectar

This recipe is a better version of the typical West Coast cedar plank salmon. Cooking the salmon in the cedar sheath – a technique borrowed from our indigenous Native forefathers – imparts more smoked cedar flavour. A timeless classic.

Wild Sockeye Salmon in Cedar Sheath

1 tbsp sesame oil

2 tbsp soy sauce

¼ cup chives

4 sheets cedar veneer, ⅙-inch thick, cut to 4-inch by 6-inch

4 strips cedar veneer, ⅙-inch thick, cut to ½-inch by 2-inch

4 4-oz fresh wild sockeye salmon fillets

The cedar veneer must be non-treated. It's available at lumber or building supply stores.

Mix sesame oil, soy sauce, and chives and coat salmon fillets and cedar veneer.

Place salmon in the middle of a larger piece of cedar. Bring the two long sides up to enclose fillet. With a sharp knife, make a small slice in the two ends of the cedar. Insert a smaller piece of cedar through the holes to seal the pouch. Repeat process with other salmon fillets.

Grill salmon in cedar pouch until medium rare to medium, about 2 minutes per side.

Cedar Gelée Glazed Baby Vegetables

2 cups chicken stock

2 tbsp cedar gelée

4 tbsp butter

8 small summer squash, patty pan variety

8 baby carrots

8 baby beets

12 snap peas

salt and pepper to taste

⅛ cup rehydrated Hijiki seaweed

Cedar gelée is a Quebec
specialty, available at
gourmet grocery stores.

Combine chicken stock, cedar gelée, butter, squash, carrots, and beets in a pan and simmer until all the liquid is reduced.

Add snap peas and season to taste.

Finish with Hijiki seaweed and set in warm place.

Apricot Fig Riesling Nectar

6 dried figs

12 dried apricots

3 cups plum wine

6 cups white wine

1 vanilla bean

¼ cup lemon juice

3 cups apricot brandy

Combine all ingredients and reduce by half.

Strain sauce and reserve apricots and figs. Dice apricots and figs and return to finished sauce.

To Plate: Place salmon in cedar at the side of the plate and arrange grilled vegetables in the centre, next to the salmon. On the other side of the plate, place a couple of dried apricots and figs. Warm the Apricot Fig Riesling Nectar in a pan and finish with a knob of butter. Drizzle around the plate.

Serves 4

Beverage Pairing: **Dry Riesling**

Grilled Tropical Fruit Kebabs with Yogurt and Ice Wine Dipping Sauce

Use fruits that will stand up to grilling, like watermelon, honeydew melon, cantaloupe (in other words, the melon family), pineapple, strawberries, and pitted fruits such as nectarines, apricots, plums, apples, and cherries. All three yogurt sauces also work well with muesli, waffles, pancakes, and French toast.

Soak a package of bamboo skewers in water overnight. Skewer a selection of fruit and grill. Serve with dipping sauce of choice.

Dipping Sauce #1

1 cup paneer (see page 21)
2 oz ice wine, or liqueur of choice

Dipping Sauce #2

1 cup paneer (see page 21)
2 tbsp pomegranate molasses
3 tbsp honey of choice

Dipping Sauce #3

1 cup paneer (see page 21)
⅛ tsp almond extract
1 tbsp buckwheat honey
⅛ cup toasted unsalted almonds, chopped
4 sprigs fresh mint, chopped

Serves 4

Beverage Pairing: Ice Wine/Muscat Moscato d'Asti

Pistachio-Crusted Warmed Brie with Gingered Biscotti, Blackberry Coulis, and Rosemary Nectar

Gingered Biscotti

¼ cup softened unsalted butter

1 cup brown sugar

2 eggs

2 tbsp molasses

2 cups all-purpose flour

1½ tsp baking powder

½ tsp salt

1 tbsp freshly ground ginger

2 tbsp powdered ginger

1 tbsp cinnamon

1 tbsp nutmeg

Preheat oven to 350°F.

In a large mixing bowl, cream butter, sugar, eggs, and molasses. In a separate bowl, sift all dry ingredients together. Add to creamed mixture.

Roll into a log on a lightly-floured surface. Place log on a cookie sheet and bake in oven for ½ hour. Let cool slightly then slice on the bias into ½-inch thick cookies. Turn oven down to 200°F.

Put cookies back on sheet and bake again, turning once, until dry, about 10 minutes.

Blackberry Coulis

1 cup fresh (or frozen) blackberries

½ cup sugar

⅛ cup blackberry vinegar (optional)

In pot on medium heat, simmer blackberries with sugar and vinegar for 15 minutes. The berries should be softened and release their juice. Purée and strain. Set aside.

To make rosemary nectar, mix ½ cup wildflower honey (or your favourite fragrant honey), 1 sprig fresh rosemary (stems on to infuse with flavour), and ½ cup pistachio nuts, lightly toasted and ground. In a pot on medium heat, heat honey and rosemary until it starts to bubble. Pour into container and let stand 24 hours.

To Plate: Crust both sides of an 8 oz wedge of double cream French brie with ground pistachio nuts. Bake on parchment paper-lined baking sheet in a 350° oven for 5 minutes until cheese starts to ooze and melt. Serve on a platter with a drizzle of coulis, rosemary nectar (see sidebar), and gingered biscotti on the side.

Serves 4

Beverage Pairing: **Aged Ruby Port**

Forkin'
Fiesta

Pomme Tomaquette

A traditional accompaniment to any Spanish tapas or antipasto platter.

1 loaf good-quality crusty bread

extra-virgin olive oil

1 bulb peeled garlic cloves

6 very ripe vine-ripened tomatoes

Pinch sea salt

Preheat oven to 400°F.

Cut bread into 1-inch thick slices and drizzle with olive oil. Rub each slice of bread with garlic cloves.

Crush tomatoes through a strainer so that only the juice remains. Coat bread pieces with juice. Season lightly with salt.

Bake in oven for 10-15 minutes. The outside of the bread should be crunchy; the inside should be warmed through.

Serves 4

Beverage Pairing: **Faugeres**

TKO Mussels

The mussel dishes in this book come from the classic *moules et frites*, a standard in Belgium, and one I discovered on a trip there. Because the Belgians are the world's leading beer aficionados, Belgian cooks often incorporate beer into their recipes. My twist on the classic *moules et frites* contains beer, habañero pepper (the hottest pepper in the world), and Kaffir lime leaves, which add a fragrant aroma. Chile and beer, over the years, has also become a classic combination. I have named these mussels TKO, or technical knock out, for the flavour and heat they generate. At the Bins, we like to serve our mussels with grilled focaccia, instead of the classic frites, so the customers can dip their bread in the flavourful broth.

2 tbsp extra-virgin olive oil

2 cloves garlic, finely diced

1 shallot, finely diced

1 whole habañero chile, or Scotch bonnet, cut in half (see page 16)

1 lb fresh mussels, bearded, rinsed, and cleaned (see page 23)

6 oz honey lager beer

6 fresh (or frozen) Kaffir lime leaves

1 tbsp butter

In a large saucepan with a lid, on high heat, lightly sauté garlic, shallot, and habañero in olive oil. Add mussels, stirring quickly. Add beer and Kaffir lime leaves.

Cover and let mussels steam for 2 minutes. Stir mussels. Add butter. Cover again for 2 minutes. Discard any unopened mussels.

Serves 4

Beverage Pairing: Well-hopped pale ale

Paella Valencia

1 tbsp garlic, chopped

2 tbsp olive oil

3 cups long grain white rice

4 cups chicken stock

1 pinch saffron (approx. 15 strands)

1 tsp paprika

2 spicy chorizo sausages, chopped

1 lb dark chicken meat (legs or thighs)

1 cup white wine

1 cup tomato concassé (see page 45)

½ lb clams, cleaned

½ lb mussels, bearded, rinsed and cleaned (see page 23)

½ lb prawns, shelled, deveined and cleaned (see page 23)

½ lb squid, spine and tentacles removed, and cleaned (see page 23)

1 cup fresh peas

salt and pepper to taste

In a very large saucepan, with a tight fitting lid, on medium heat, sweat garlic in olive oil until translucent.

Add rice, stirring to coat with garlic and olive oil. Add chicken stock, saffron, and paprika. Raise heat to high and bring to a boil. Stir rice thoroughly. Reduce heat to medium. Cover and cook until rice is about half done, about 15 minutes.

Add all remaining ingredients, including wine. If rice seems dry, add more chicken stock.

Cover and continue to cook on medium heat until chicken and seafood are cooked, and there is just a small amount of liquid left, about 15 minutes.

Serves 4

Beverage Pairing: **Albarino**

Argentinean Peel-and-Eat Sizzling Garlic Side Stripe or Spot Prawns with Roasted Habañero and Pineapple Pan Dressing

Bib required for this dish if eaten properly. Don't forget to share! It's not nice to be shellfish. Ooh, stinky! Sorry. Had to.

2 roasted habañero peppers (seeds optional) (see page 16)

1 fresh pineapple, cubed

1 lb local spot prawns (or other red-shelled prawns)

6 cloves garlic, peeled and minced

3 tbsp olive oil

¼ cup dry white wine

salt to taste

½ bunch fresh Thai basil, chopped

⅛ cup butter, melted (optional)

In a saucepan on medium heat, combine pineapple and habañero peppers and reduce by ½. Remove from heat and, in a blender, blend until smooth. Let cool, strain, and set aside.

In a large skillet on high heat, sauté prawns and garlic in olive oil for 1 minute. Add white wine, salt, and basil. Cook until prawn shells start to separate, about 2-3 minutes. Do not overcook or prawns will become rubbery.

To Plate: Place prawns in middle of plate, pour sauce over top, and drizzle with melted butter, if desired.

Serves 4

Beverage Pairing: Off-dry German Reisling

3-Citrus Halibut Ceviche, Gazpacho Vinaigrette, and Avocado Fritters

3-Citrus Halibut Ceviche

4 3-oz halibut fillets, thinly sliced

juice of 1 orange

juice of 1 lemon

juice of 1 lime

dash of sugar

1 jalapeño pepper, finely diced (optional) (see page 16)

few sprigs fresh cilantro or flat leaf (Italian) parsley

In a mixing bowl, combine all ingredients, tossing every few minutes, for about 15 minutes. The acid lightly cooks the fish. Once fish turns lightly opaque, ceviche is ready to serve.

Avocado Fritters

½ cup tempura flour

4 tbsp cold water

black sesame seeds, toasted (optional)

1 ripe avocado, cut into 8 slices

salt and pepper to taste

canola oil for deep-frying

In a mixing bowl, loosely combine tempura batter and water and leave lumpy. For added flavour and presentation, add toasted black sesame seeds to the batter.

Season avocado slices with salt and pepper and dip in batter. If batter is too thick, add more water.

In a deep-fat fryer, heated to 360°F. Carefully drop in fritters and let fry for about 1 minute or until they float to the surface. Absorb excess oil by placing fritters on a paper towel.

Gazpacho Vinaigrette

1 red pepper, seeds removed and roughly chopped

1 red onion, roughly chopped

1 long English cucumber, roughly chopped

1 ripe Roma tomato, roughly chopped

2 tbsp extra-virgin olive oil

4 tbsp red wine vinegar

sea salt and white pepper to taste

In a food processor or blender, purée vegetables to make a juice. Strain and reserve liquid. Combine with olive oil, red wine vinegar, and salt and pepper. Can be made up to 24 hours in advance.

To Plate: Place slices of ceviche on plate and drizzle with gazpacho vinaigrette. Place fritters to the side.

Serves 4

Beverage Pairing: Semillon or Semillon/Chardonnay, BC Pinôt Gris (for fritters)

Chicken Mole with Roast Sweet Bell Pepper and Toasted Pumpkin Seed Rice Pilaf

I believe mole – a blend of chocolate, chiles, and spices – originates from Mexico. Like curry, it has many variations, depending on the region. I think you will find this version appealing and a good introduction to the world of mole. Removing the seeds from the chiles will lower the heat level.

chicken pieces: 4 legs, 4 thighs, 4 breasts

3 tbsp olive oil

4½ cups chicken stock (see page 18)

3 tbsp olive oil

8 Roma tomatoes, roughly chopped

1 onion, diced

8 kinds of chiles, dried and fresh (your choice)

⅛ cup cinnamon powder

½ cup ground coriander

½ cup ground cumin

½ cup garlic, minced

½ cup cocoa powder

Preheat oven to 350°F.

In a large saucepan, brown the chicken pieces in olive oil. Deglaze with chicken stock. Transfer pieces to large baking pan and roast in oven for 30-45 minutes.

In a separate saucepan, lightly sweat off remaining ingredients except cocoa powder in olive oil until onions are translucent. When tomatoes start to break down to a sauce, add the cocoa.

Toasted Pumpkin Seed Rice Pilaf

½ white onion, diced

¼ cup butter

2 cups basmati rice, rinsed

salt and pepper to taste

3 cups chicken stock (see page 18) or water with 3 bay leaves

1½ cups pumpkin seeds, toasted

In a saucepan with a lid, on medium heat, sauté onion in butter until translucent. Add rice and stir to coat. Salt and pepper to taste. Add stock and bring to a boil. Cover tightly and cook on low heat for 15-20 minutes.

Turn off heat, but do not lift lid! Let stand 15 minutes. Add toasted pumpkin seeds.

Serves 4

Beverage Pairing: Old-world-style Valpolicella

Pan-Seared Wentzel Duck Breast, White Chocolate/Chile Johnny Cakes, Warm Pancetta Frisée Salad and Oven-Dried Cranberry Sauce

1 orange rind

zest of 1 lemon

1 tsp cinnamon or ground cassia buds

1 tsp coarse sea salt

freshly ground black pepper to taste

4 medium-sized duck breasts

1 tbsp canola oil

Preheat oven to 350°F.

In a mortar and pestle, grind together salt, pepper, orange rind, lemon zest, and cinnamon or cassia buds.

To prepare duck, use a sharp knife to make a cross-hatch pattern on the thick fatty side of each breast. Liberally rub ground spices deep into the cross-hatch openings.

In an ovenproof frying pan on high heat, heat canola oil. Place duck breasts skin side down in pan. Cook for 2-3 minutes. Render (pour fat from pan). Continue cooking duck, skin-side down, for 3 more minutes. Render fat again. Place frying pan in oven until duck is medium-rare to medium, about 8-10 minutes.

Oven-Dried Cranberry Sauce

2 cups frozen cranberries

2 small shallots, diced

2 cups frozen raspberries

2 cups raspberry wine

2 cups veal stock or 4 oz demi-glace (see page 17)

salt and pepper to taste

1 tbsp butter

Place frozen cranberries in a 170°F oven until dry, about 5-6 hours.

In a small pot, combine shallots, frozen raspberries, and raspberry wine.

Simmer until reduced by half. Strain. Add oven-dried cranberries and demi-glace and bring to a boil. Salt and pepper to taste, if needed, and finish with butter just before serving.

Johnny Cakes

¾ cups flour

1¼ cups blue cornmeal

¼ cup yellow cornmeal

¼ cup sugar

¼ tsp baking powder

¼ tsp salt

¼ cup chopped white chocolate

¼ cup hominy

⅛ cup yellow onion

¼ cup canola oil

1 tsp ground chipotle pepper

¾ cup milk

1 egg

Preheat oven to 350°F.

In a mixing bowl, combine flour, cornmeal, sugar, baking powder, salt, and chocolate.

In a food processor, mix hominy, onion, canola oil, and chipotle. Add milk and egg, and pulse.

Add wet to dry ingredients and pour into small non-stick 3" x 2" loaf pans (or use standard-sized loaf pan and portion when serving). Bake until skewer comes out clean, about 20-30 minutes.

Warm Pancetta Frisée Salad

¼ cup pancetta, diced

2 small shallots, diced

1 large head frisée or curly endive

2 sprigs fresh tarragon leaves, chopped

3 tbsp champagne vinegar or ver jus

1 tsp ground black pepper

In a hot frying pan, sauté pancetta until fat leaches out and pancetta is crispy. Add shallots, sauté until translucent (about 1 minute). Cut bottom off frisee so stalks are separate and add to pan. Add all other ingredients and toss frisee until coated and lightly wilted.

To Plate: Arrange the salad in the centre of each plate and place the duck leg leaning on one side. Place a slice of Johnny Cake opposite. Drizzle some extra dressing around and garnish with fennel strands.

Serves 4

Beverage Pairing: California/New Zealand Pinôt Noir

Yucatan Steak Rub TV Dinner with Pineapple Tamarind Salsa, Pumpkin Seed Poblano Pepper Bannock, and Southwest Succotash

We serve this dish in a Japanese-style Bento Box with 4-5 different sections: hence the name TV dinner. This blend of Native American flavours with traditional Mexican ones creates a fun and colourful dish.

1 lb flank steak, cut into 4 4-oz pieces

2 tbsp achiote paste

½ tsp garlic powder

1 morita chile with seeds, toasted (see page 16)

1 ancho chile, seeded (see page 16)

1 guajillo chile, seeded (see page 16)

½ tsp ground cumin

¼ tsp ground allspice

salt and pepper to taste

The day before, score flank steak. Combine seasonings and rub into scores. Cover and refrigerate for 24 hours.

Salt and pepper to taste. Grill until medium-rare, about 2 minutes each side.

Pineapple Tamarind Salsa

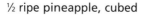

½ ripe pineapple, cubed

½ red onion, chopped

½ red bell pepper, chopped

1 jalapeño, with seeds, chopped (see page 16)

½ bunch fresh cilantro, chopped

¼ cup tamarind pulp

In a large mixing bowl, combine all ingredients. Cover and marinate in
refrigerator for 2 to 4 hours prior to serving.

Southwest Succotash

½ cup bacon, cubed

1 white onion, diced

4 ears fresh corn kernels

1 cup fresh green beans

1 red pepper, diced

1 cup cherry tomatoes

¼ cup sunflower seeds, toasted and ground

salt and pepper to taste

In a skillet on high heat, cook bacon until crispy. Remove. Do not drain fat.
To the same pan, add onion, corn, beans, red pepper, and sauté until *al
dente*. Add tomatoes, sunflower seeds, and salt and pepper. Cook over
high heat stirring for 2 minutes and serve.

Pumpkin Seed Poblano Pepper Bannock

2 cups masa harina

1½ cup all-purpose flour

1 tsp baking powder

1 tsp salt

1½ cups water

⅛ + ¼ cup poblano peppers, chopped

⅛ + ¼ cup pumpkin seeds, toasted

vegetable oil for deep-frying

In a mixing bowl, combine the masa harina, flour, baking powder, and salt. Add water and mix dough until it comes together in a ball. Add poblano peppers and pumpkin seeds. Knead dough until supple but not sticking to your skin. Wrap in saran wrap and let rest in fridge for 1 hour. Lightly knead rested dough. Tear off dough balls approximately 2" in diameter. Press dough balls flat into a circle and roll with rolling pin, adding more flour if dough sticks to pin.

In a deep-fat fryer at 350°F, fry until dough puffs up. Another option is to brush tops of bannock with oil and grill like tortillas.

Makes about 24.

To Plate: Let meat rest. Slice into strips. Serve taco-style in bannock along with succotash and salsa.

Serves 4

Beverage Pairing: Chilean Carmanere

Albondigas (Spanish Meatballs) with Sherry Sauce

3 cloves garlic, finely diced

3 shallots, finely diced

1 tsp olive oil

1 lb ground lamb

1 lb ground pork

3 eggs

1½ cups breadcrumbs

1 tbsp Spanish paprika

salt and pepper to taste

⅛ tsp cumin

pinch of ground cloves

1 bunch fresh oregano, chopped

Preheat oven to 400°F.

In a saucepan on medium heat, sauté garlic and shallots in olive oil until translucent. Do not burn. Let cool.

In a large mixing bowl, combine lamb, pork, and eggs. Add all remaining ingredients including garlic and shallots. Using your hands, mix and form into 1-inch balls. Meatballs should be moist, not dry and falling apart.

Place meatballs on a baking tray lined with parchment paper. Bake in oven for approximately 20 minutes. Check after 15 minutes; meatballs should be lightly crisped on the outside, and moist and just-cooked throughout.

Sherry Sauce

1 tbsp olive oil

2 carrots, chopped

1 stalk celery, chopped

1 medium onion, chopped

3 cups veal stock (see page 17)

2 cups dry red sherry

⅛ cup cold butter cubes

In a medium saucepan on high heat, heat olive oil and lightly caramelize carrots, celery, and onion. Add veal stock and sherry and reduce by ½.

Place in food processor, and purée. Pour through a strainer, then back into saucepan and reduce puréed sauce by ⅓, until it becomes dark and syrupy. When ready to serve, stir in cold butter cubes.

To Plate: Serve platter-style. Place meatballs, with sauce, in centre of platter. Serve with *Pomme Tomaquette* (see page 66) like an open-faced meatball sandwich.

Serves 4

Beverage Pairing: Argentinian Malbec

Spanish High-Country Beef Short Ribs and White Bean Cassoulet

This is the Spanish rebuttal to Osso Buco. Loosen your belts!

8 ancho chiles

2 tsp black pepper

1 tsp salt

12 beef short ribs

2 carrots, peeled and diced

2 onions, peeled and diced

½ head celery, diced

3 ripe tomatoes, diced

3 red peppers, roasted, deseeded, and julienned

½ bottle cooking sherry

1 litre veal stock (see page 18)

8 bay leaves

1 sprig fresh thyme

2 whole garlic bulbs, crushed

Preheat oven to 350°F.

In a mortar and pestle, grind together 2 of the 8 ancho chiles, black pepper, and salt. Rub ribs with mix.

In a roasting pan on high heat, sear ribs on both sides. Remove from pan.

Using the same pan, add vegetables. Deglaze with sherry.

Place ribs back in pan and pour in enough veal stock to cover ribs.

Place rest of ancho chiles, bay leaves, thyme, and crushed garlic into pan. Cover with foil and braise in oven until tender, about 1½ hours.

White Bean Cassoulet

½ lb back bacon, chopped

6 chorizo sausages, chopped at angles

1 pork hock

6 carrots, roughly chopped

12 bay leaves

3 large white onions, roughly chopped

3 carrots, roughly chopped

½ head celery, roughly chopped

5 sprigs fresh thyme in cheesecloth

1 cup roasted garlic (see page 15)

5 pasilla chiles

black peppercorns in cheesecloth

2 whole tomatoes

10 cups presoaked white beans

In a saucepan, sweat all ingredients except peppercorns, tomatoes, and beans. When vegetables are ¼ cooked, add water to barely cover and simmer for 10 minutes. Add peppercorns. Add whole tomatoes and remove just when they start to break.

Add beans and cook until done. Pick out chiles.

To Plate: **Serve platter-style.**

Serves 4

Beverage Pairing: **Zinfandel**

Ibarra Mexican Chocolate and Bailey's Crème Brûlée

1 3-oz disk Ibarra chocolate

½ litre whipping cream

2 oz Bailey's liqueur

6 egg yolks

¼ cup white sugar

Using a double boiler, melt chocolate. In a separate pot, heat the whipping cream and Bailey's just to boiling point.

In a large bowl, whisk the egg yolks and sugar together. Slowly add the chocolate and cream mixture, being careful not to cook the eggs.

Strain the mixture and place into ramekins in a *bain-marie* (see page 21). Cover and cook until set, about 1½ hours. They should quiver slightly when shaken.

Remove from water bath and let cool. Refrigerate overnight.

To caramelize the tops, sprinkle with white sugar and, using either a blowtorch or the broiler in the oven, brown the sugar.

Serves 4

Beverage Pairing: **Bingria (see page 86)**

Warm Banana in Phyllo à la "Binana" Split

4 bananas, peeled

¼ cup brown sugar

1 tbsp cinnamon

1 oz dark rum

4 sheets phyllo dough (see sidebar)

¼ cup clarified butter (see page 21)

1 cup whipping cream

¼ cup mascarpone cheese

2 drops pure vanilla extract

2 tbsp icing sugar

When working with phyllo, thaw in fridge overnight. Try to work quickly and keep reserved sheets covered with a damp kitchen towel.

Marinate bananas in brown sugar, cinnamon, and rum for 15 minutes.

Preheat oven to 350°F.

Brush 1 sheet of phyllo with butter and fold it over. Place marinated banana at edge of phyllo and roll, brushing with butter every roll, until you have a cylinder. Butter to close cylinder.

Bake cylinders in centre of a parchment-lined baking sheet until phyllo is crispy, turning over once.

In the meantime, whip 1 cup whipping cream until soft peaks form.

In a mixing bowl, combine mascarpone cheese, vanilla extract, and icing sugar. Combine with whipped cream and whip until stiff peaks form.

To Plate: Serve with a dollop of whipped cheese, chocolate or caramel sauce, chopped hazelnuts or pecans, and seasonal fresh fruits.

Serves 4

Beverage Pairing: Tawny Port

Bingria

This is our better-than-sex version of sangria, or so we've been told.

2 medium nectarines, sliced

½ pint frozen blueberries, cubed

½ pint frozen raspberries, cubed

½ 750-ml bottle late harvest Vidal or any late harvest wine

½ 750-ml bottle Columbia valley raspberry wine

⅓ 750-ml bottle plum wine

¼ 750-ml bottle apricot brandy

2 750-ml bottles dry red wine

1 orange slice (garnish)

1 brandy straw (garnish)

Aranciata (Italian orange soda) (optional)

In a 4-quart container, combine all ingredients except orange, brandy straw, and Aranciata.

Serve over ice in tall tumblers. Garnish with orange slice and brandy straw.

Top each glass with splash of Aranciata.

Serves 12-24

East/West

Smoked Chicken Udon Noodle Soup

Reward yourself by smoking your own chicken (see page 24). It's a far superior product, and once you get used to using your home smoker, you will discover the ease and magic of the multitude of pairings you can smoke and enjoy at home. This dish is a kind of melting pot so to speak: a blend of Chinese egg swirl soup, Italian *straciatella*, and good old-fashioned chicken noodle soup. No excuses not to make this one. Too simple for words, it will become a comfort-food favourite.

4½ cups chicken stock (see page 18)

1 cup smoked chicken meat, shredded

1 package precooked udon noodles

¼ cup Marsala wine

salt and pepper to taste

3 eggs

1 bunch chives, chopped (optional)

In a stockpot on high heat, bring chicken stock to boil. Add chicken, noodles, and wine.

Bring back to boil until heated throughout, about 1-2 minutes. Salt and pepper to taste.

In a bowl, whisk 3 eggs together. Stir eggs into soup, and then remove from heat.

Portion soup into bowls. Sprinkle with chives.

Serves 4

Beverage Pairing: **French or Spanish Rosé**

Green Papaya Salad

A salad version of the classic Thai noodle dish, Pad Thai. A fresh, healthy, and tasty salad perfect to accompany grilled meats, fish, or poultry, and good for these low-carb days. With a mandoline you will be able to spin the carrots to a fine noodle.

For Salad:

1 cup red cabbage, finely julienned

1 cup carrots, finely julienned

2 cups green papayas, finely julienned

10 leaves fresh Thai basil

10 leaves fresh cilantro, roughly chopped

10 leaves fresh mint

1 head butter lettuce (for plating)

1 Asian pear, sliced (for plating)

4 kumquats, sliced (for plating)

½ cup roughly ground peanuts, toasted or ½ cup garlic chips (garnish)

For Dressing:

2 tbsp white sugar

4 tsp sambal chile

4 tsp fish sauce

4 cups fresh lime juice

¾ cups garlic

2¼ cups peanut oil

In a blender, mix dressing ingredients, making sure that garlic is fully incorporated and that no chunks remain.

In a large bowl, vigorously toss vegetables, papaya, and herbs in the dressing until they are coated.

To Plate: Separate about 2-3 butter lettuce leaves and arrange on plate to form 3 points. Place dressed papaya salad in the centre. Garnish with Asian pears, placed around the edge of the plate. Place kumquats on top of Asian pear wedges. Sprinkle with peanuts or garlic chips.

Serves 2 as an entrée, 4 as an appetizer

Beverage Pairing: **Pinôt Blanc**

East/West Crab Cakes with
Burnt-Orange Chipotle Sauce

The inspiration for this recipe comes from my love of Asian and southwestern New Mexican cuisine. Many types of crab can be found on the west coast of British Columbia. Some are sweeter than others; some are saltier. The chipotle pepper, which is actually a smoked and cured jalapeño pepper, is the southwestern influence and oranges and tangerines are often found in Asian cuisine. This dish is still a top server at the Bins; it's been on the menu every day for 6 years running.

½ medium red onion, diced

2 tbsp olive oil

1 red bell pepper, diced

1 lb fresh Dungeness crab meat (or local crab meat)

6 sprigs cilantro, chopped

1 large egg

½ cup mayonnaise

1 tbsp sesame oil

1 tsp sea salt

½ tsp white pepper

1 tsp Szechuan peppercorns, toasted and ground

juice of 1 lemon

2 cups panko

3 tbsp water

1 egg (for dipping)

½ cup all-purpose flour

1 tbsp olive oil

1 tbsp unsalted butter

Preheat oven to 400°F.

In a saucepan on medium heat, sauté onions in olive oil for 1 minute. Reduce heat to medium-low and sweat onions until translucent.

Transfer onions to a bowl. Let cool. Bring pan back up to high heat and sauté red peppers until lightly caramelized, about 2 minutes. Turn heat down again and cook until peppers are softened, about 5 minutes.

Add peppers to the bowl of onions. When onions and pepper have cooled, add crab meat, cilantro, egg, mayonnaise, all seasonings, lemon juice, sesame oil, and ½ cup panko. Mix until well combined. The mixture should stick together without falling apart as you form cakes. If necessary, you can adjust the mayonnaise and panko quantities to compensate.

Using your hands, or a 2-inch round pastry cutter, form cakes.

In a separate bowl, whisk 1 egg and 3 tbsp water until frothy. Place flour and the rest of the panko in two separate bowls. Lightly coat cakes in flour. Dip into egg wash, then coat with panko flakes.

In an ovenproof saucepan on medium heat, combine 1 tbsp unsalted butter and 1 tbsp olive oil. Once butter has melted, cook crab cakes until lightly golden, about 3 minutes. Turn cakes and place in oven for 5 minutes. Cakes should be golden brown on both sides and warmed in the middle.

Burnt-Orange Chipotle Sauce

½ can orange concentrate, defrosted

2 tbsp ground chipotle peppers

1 cup dry white wine

3 tbsp unsalted butter

In a saucepan on medium heat, whisk orange juice until slightly caramelized. The juice should turn a rust colour and taste slightly tart. Add the chipotle pepper, reduce heat to low, and simmer for 10 minutes. Finish sauce by adding wine and butter. If you're on a diet, you can omit this last step and still have a full-flavoured sauce.

To Plate Or Not to Plate, That is the Question. In other words, use your imagination on this one. Just don't pour sauce over the crab cakes because it will make them soggy. Baby bok choy sautéed with a dash of sesame oil, lime juice, and salt and pepper makes a nice side dish.

Serves 4

Beverage Pairing: B.C. Gewürztraminer

Coconut Milk and Garam Masala Mussels

Curry powders are like signatures. There are many combinations and each one comes from its own village or region of India, and varies depending on what spices are available. Can you imagine walking the distance from Vancouver to Tijuana, Mexico to trade 1 cup of black peppercorns for 1 cup of cinnamon and back again just to finish your curry powder? Exactly. This is why there are so many variations.

Garam masala tends to be more aromatic and less spicy, depending on which village you visit, but for the most part it's cardamom, cloves, cinnamon, and mustard seeds and it blends wonderfully with coconut milk and the juice of the mussels. The chile flakes give it the gentle, or not so gentle, kick needed to round out the dish.

This one needs a spoon or bread or fries, but most of all it needs you.

¼ cup leek, white part only, julienned

pinch of red chile flakes

1 tbsp garam masala or 1 tsp curry powder

2 tbsp extra-virgin olive oil

1 lb fresh mussels, bearded, rinsed, and cleaned (see page 23)

3 oz dry white wine

4 oz coconut milk

In a large skillet with a lid, lightly sauté leeks, chile flakes, and garam masala in olive oil. Add remaining ingredients. Cover and let steam until all mussels have opened, 3–5 minutes. Discard any unopened mussels.

Serves 1 as an entrée, 4 as an appetizer

Pan-Seared Squid in Lime, Chile, and Garlic Sauce

A much nicer tasting (I think) version of calamari. No fuss. No muss. No crust. No deep frying! Squid is readily available and inexpensive. This dish will convert even the staunchest calamari hater, or else it's chicken knuckles for you, buddy!

8 medium squids, cleaned (see page 23)

⅛ cup onion, chopped

⅛ red onion, finely diced

6 cloves garlic, chopped

1 tsp chile oil (see page 14)

3 fresh Thai (or serrano) chiles

salt and pepper to taste

2 tbsp olive or canola oil

juice of 2 limes

1 tbsp oyster sauce

1 bunch scallions made into flowers (see sidebar)

To make scallion flowers, cut the white ends of the scallions into 1-inch lengths. Make many cross patterns about ¼-inch deep on ends of white parts. Submerge in ice cold water, and in about 5 minutes the onions will look like flowers.

Cut cleaned squid into ½-inch thick rings. In a large mixing bowl, combine squid, onions, chile oil, garlic, Thai chiles, salt, and pepper. Marinate for 1 hour at room temperature.

In a cast iron or heavy-bottomed pan on high, heat olive oil. Add squid mixture and salt and cook, stirring, for 1 minute. Stir in lime juice and oyster sauce. Be careful not to overcook, as squid will become rubbery and chewy.

To Plate: Pour onto serving tray and garnish with the scallions.

Serves 4

Beverage Pairing: Pinôt Grigio

Roast Wild Atlantic Salmon and Scallops with Hot and Sour Broth and Pacific Rim Agnolloti

Always use wild salmon, when available, because they are hormone and drug free. They eat a diet of wild plankton and critters and have a higher fat content and scads more flavour. Help support responsible sustainable fishing, please!

This dish is a substantial and palate-pleasing fish entrée. You can also omit the fish and scallops and serve as a soup starter if desired. Enjoy this recipe courtesy the right side of my brain.

Hot and Sour Broth

9 cups halibut stock (see page 19)

1 smoked salmon head (see page 24)

¼ cup fresh ginger, peeled and sliced

2 Thai bird chiles, chopped

⅓ cup rice wine vinegar

2 tbsp salt

2 tbsp sweet chile sauce

2 tbsp lemon juice

1 tbsp fish sauce

8 Kaffir lime leaves

1 stalk lemongrass

In a large stockpot, slowly simmer all ingredients for 30 minutes, skimming any residue that rises to the top. Carefully strain through a fine sieve and discard the solids.

Roast Salmon and Scallops

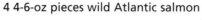

4 4-6-oz pieces wild Atlantic salmon

2 tbsp olive oil

8 large scallops

salt and pepper to taste

Preheat oven to 375°F.

In an ovenproof saucepan, caramelize salmon in oil on one side. Flip salmon and place pan in oven until fish is cooked, about 5 minutes. Remove salmon and set aside.

In the same pan, back on high heat, sear scallops until done, about 2 minutes each side.

Pacific Rim Agnolloti

For Filling:

3 white onions, sliced

1 tbsp unsalted butter

1 tsp white sugar

3 cups butternut squash, diced

1 tbsp unsalted butter

¼ tsp ground coriander

¼ tsp ground cinnamon

3 cups shitake mushrooms, sliced

1 tbsp unsalted butter

1 tbsp sesame oil

1 tbsp white sesame seeds

3 red bell peppers, roasted and diced (see page 15)

¼ tsp ground Szechuan pepper

¼ cup green onions, sliced

¼ cup cilantro, chopped

2 tbsp soy sauce

salt and white pepper to taste

In a saucepan on medium heat, caramelize the onions in butter and sugar.

In a separate pan, roast the butternut squash in 1 tbsp butter. Add coriander and cinnamon and roast until squash is soft and lightly mashed.

Again, using 1 tbsp of butter, sauté the shitake mushrooms with sesame oil and seeds.

In a large bowl, combine all ingredients and adjust seasonings. Let cool.

For Dough:

1½ cup all-purpose flour

2 eggs

1½ tbsp olive oil

1½ tbsp water

Sift flour. In a food processor fitted with the dough blade attachment, blend eggs, oil, and 1 tbsp of water. Add the sifted flour and start the machine. Blend the dough until it comes together in a ball, adding the remaining ½ tbsp water, if necessary.

Remove dough and knead it into a smooth ball. Wrap in plastic and let rest for 30 minutes.

Roll out 2 sheets in a pasta machine to #6 thickness.

To make Agnolloti, cut the pasta sheets into 3-inch squares. Place 2 tbsp of filling in centre of each. Brush edges with water, then place another square on top and seal the edges.

Cook the Agnolloti in a large pot of boiling salted water for 3 minutes.

Makes about 12 Agnolloti.

To Plate: Place 1 or 2 Agnolloti in a large shallow soup bowl and ladle the hot and sour broth over. Place the roast salmon on top of Agnolloti. Skewer the scallops with a small bamboo skewer and place in the salmon so that it stands up. Sprinkle chives over exposed top portion of skewer and drizzle lightly with sesame oil, if desired.

Serves 4

Beverage Pairing: Chenin Blanc

Skillet-Roasted Sablefish with Plum Wine and Madagascar Peppercorn Sauce, Lobster Fumet Potato Stack, and Caramelized Fennel

Chilean sea bass, the fish used originally for this recipe, has now become endangered. Pacific sablefish, a.k.a. Alaska black cod, is a more than worthy substitution and has the same butter-rich texture.

4 4-oz sablefish pieces

2 tbsp olive oil

4 tsp green peppercorns

½ cup Japanese plum wine

⅛ cup butter

In a skillet on high heat, sear sablefish in oil. Remove fillets. Place peppercorns in the pan. Add plum wine and deglaze. Stir in butter to finish.

Lobster Fumet Potato Stack

For lobster stock:

2 lbs lobster shells (available from you local fishmonger)

1 yellow onion, roughly chopped

1 leek, white part only, roughly chopped

1 red bell pepper, roughly chopped

¼ head celery, roughly chopped

1 carrot, roughly chopped

2 tomatoes, roughly chopped

½ bulb garlic, peeled

1 bay leaf

⅛ cup Pernod

12 strands saffron

Roast shells and all ingredients except Pernod and saffron in a 400°F oven until vegetables are caramelized, about ½ hour. Deglaze with Pernod.

Cover with water. Boil at medium heat until reduced by ⅓. Add saffron and strain.

For Potatoes:

8 russet potatoes, peeled and diced

¼ cup butter

pinch Spanish paprika

In a skillet on high heat, sauté potatoes in butter until browned on all sides.

Pour lobster stock into pan and stir until potatoes absorb the liquid. Add paprika for colour.

Caramelized Fennel

1 fennel bulb

⅓ cup butter

3 whole star anise

salt and pepper to taste

½ cup apple juice

Preheat oven to 400°F.

Cut fennel in 4 pieces. In a frying pan on medium heat, sear fennel in butter until golden brown. Season with salt and pepper, and add star anise. Transfer fennel to a baking dish. To the frying pan, add apple juice and deglaze pan.

Pour sauce over top of fennel and bake in oven until medium tender, about 10 minutes.

To Plate: Fill a ring mould with potatoes and stack the fish on the potatoes. Remove mould from ingredients, which should stand up on their own. Garnish with fennel and pour the sauce around the plate and on the fish.

Serves 4

Beverage Pairing: Pinôt Auxerois

Grilled Volcanic Salt-Rubbed Halibut, Roasted Crimini Mushrooms, Caramelized Kabocha Squash Salad, Rosemary Lemon Jus, and Sweet and Sour Onion Salsa

The Alea red salt and Meyer lemon are the finishing touches that bring this dish together with a fresh, fragrant flavour highlighting the crispy skin of the fish with its naturally oily interior. This dish works equally well in summer or winter. For summer, serve with vegetables *al dente* and for winter, puréed potatoes and squash.

Sweet and Sour Onion Salsa

1 cup sugar

3 cups water

2 cups white wine vinegar

2 large red onions, thinly sliced

In a saucepan over medium heat, dissolve sugar in water and white wine vinegar. Add onion slices, cover, and let pickle overnight in the fridge.

Roasted Crimini Mushrooms, Caramelized Kabocha Squash Salad

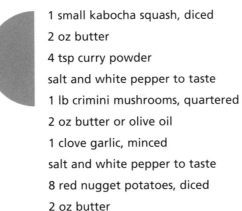

1 small kabocha squash, diced

2 oz butter

4 tsp curry powder

salt and white pepper to taste

1 lb crimini mushrooms, quartered

2 oz butter or olive oil

1 clove garlic, minced

salt and white pepper to taste

8 red nugget potatoes, diced

2 oz butter

salt and white pepper to taste

Preheat oven to 375°F.

In a large saucepan on medium heat, sauté squash in butter for about 5 minutes, adding curry powder, salt, and pepper to taste.

Transfer to a baking dish and bake in oven until fork tender, about 20 minutes. Remove from oven and let cool.

In the meantime, in a saucepan on medium heat, sauté crimini mushrooms in butter. Add garlic, and salt and pepper to taste and cook until mushrooms are done, about 5 minutes. Set aside to cool.

Finally, in an ovenproof pan, sauté potatoes in butter on medium heat. Season with salt and pepper and finish in oven until fork tender, about 20 minutes. Set aside to cool.

Combine vegetables in a large serving bowl.

Grilled Volcanic Salt-Rubbed Halibut and Rosemary Lemon Jus

4 5-oz halibut fillets

Alea red salt to taste

white pepper to taste

1 tbsp olive oil

1 tbsp butter

2 cups halibut stock (see page 19)

1 cup white wine

3 sprigs rosemary

1 tbsp Meyer lemon oil

salt and white pepper to taste

Alea red salt comes from lava beds in Hawaii where salt water collects and deposits. It is sweeter and smoother tasting than regular sea salt, plus it looks cool.

Preheat oven to 375°F.

Sprinkle fish with Alea red salt on one side, and white pepper on both sides. In a skillet on medium heat, sauté fish, salt side down, in olive oil and butter for 5 minutes. Transfer to a baking dish and bake in the oven for 5 minutes.

In the same pan you used for the fish and on medium heat, combine halibut stock, white wine, and rosemary and reduce to ½. Add lemon oil, salt, and white pepper.

To Plate: Using a ring mould, fill the ring with the salad. Remove mould from ingredients, which should now stand up nicely. Top with fish, sweet and sour onion salsa, and drizzle with rosemary lemon jus.

Serves 4

Beverage Pairing: **Australian Marsanne**

Rose Water and Lily Flower Poached Pacific Halibut, Crisp "White" Salad with Sweet Miso Dijon Dressing, Toasted Sesame Seed Dashi Reduction, and Grilled Enoki Mushrooms

This dish is pure white, and it's striking! To contradict the surreal look of the dish, it's packed with bold, exciting flavours. Artistic and freaky at the same time, with an understated elegance, The Beatles' *White Album* is the perfect background music.

Rose Water and Lily Flower Poached Pacific Halibut

2 tbsp rose water

2 cups halibut stock (see page 19)

1 cup white wine

¼ cup dried lily flowers

4 4-oz fresh Pacific halibut fillets

sea salt and white pepper to taste

In a stockpot (preferably stainless steel), combine rose water, halibut stock, wine, and lily flowers and bring to a simmer. Do not boil.

Season halibut fillets with salt and white pepper and poach in liquid at a simmer for approximately 3-3½ minutes. Remove fish.

Toasted Sesame Seed Dashi Reduction

½ sheet konbu

1 litre water

1 oz bonito flakes

In a stockpot, heat konbu in water slowly until it boils. Remove konbu with tongs. Add bonito, remove from heat, and let steep for 1 hour. Strain. In a saucepan on medium heat, reduce by ⅔.

Crisp "White" Salad

1 daikon

1 jicama

1 can sliced water chestnuts, rinsed and drained

1 bunch sui choy stems

1 Vidalia onion or white parts of a leek

1 small pkg enoki mushrooms, grilled (garnish)

Using a mandoline or a food processor fitted with the appropriate blade, julienne all vegetables except water chestnuts. Place in a bowl, add chestnuts, and toss with dressing.

Sweet Miso Dijon Dressing

¼ tsp ground Szechuan peppercorns

1 tbsp Dijon mustard

2 tbsp shiro miso paste

⅛ cup champagne vinegar

juice of ½ lemon

white pepper to taste

⅛ tbsp sesame oil

⅛ tbsp bonito flakes

½ cup grapeseed oil

In a food processor or blender, purée all ingredients except grapeseed oil. Slowly add oil and blend on medium until emulsified.

To Plate: Centre dressed salad on plate. Place halibut fillet on top. Sprinkle with salt and drizzle with dashi reduction. Garnish with toasted white sesame seeds. Place lily flowers from your poaching liquid on top of each fillet and garnish with grilled enoki mushrooms.

Serves 4

Beverage Pairing: Chablis

Grilled Tuna with 3-Citrus Indonesian Peppercorn Sauce, Basmati Rice Pudding, and Watercress Salad

Grilled Tuna, 3-Citrus Indonesian Peppercorn Sauce

2 cups water

2 tbsp tamarind paste

⅓ cup kecap manis

1 tbsp Chinese five-spice powder

1 tbsp salt

1 tbsp white pepper

1 tbsp chile flakes

1 tbsp Szechuan pepper

¼ cup white wine

juice of 2 oranges

juice of 2 limes

juice of 2 lemons

½ 3.5-oz can green peppercorns with brine

½ gram saffron

8 oz boiling water (for saffron)

1 oz apple cider

1 oz mirin

1 tbsp fresh cilantro, chopped

2 tbsp butter

4 4-oz pieces Ahi tuna

In a saucepan on medium heat, simmer all ingredients except saffron, boiling water, cider, mirin, cilantro, butter, and tuna for 15 minutes. In a small pot, boil saffron in water to make a tea. Add saffron tea, apple cider, and mirin to peppercorn sauce. Reduce. Add cilantro and butter.

In a skillet on high heat, sear tuna in splash of olive oil until rare, about 1 minute each side.

Watercress Salad

1 bunch watercress, stems removed

1 tbsp sherry vinegar

1 tbsp sesame oil

2 tbsp olive oil

sea salt to taste

In a bowl, combine ingredients and toss well.

Basmati Rice Pudding

For Rice Mixture:

1 shallot, diced

1 tsp freshly ground cumin

1 tbsp unsalted butter

1 tbsp vegetable oil

¾ cup basmati rice, rinsed

1¼ cup water

½ cinnamon stick

2 Kaffir lime leaves, crushed

½ tsp salt

½ tsp freshly ground white pepper

1 tsp freshly squeezed lemon juice

In a small pot with a tight fitting lid, sauté the shallot and cumin in
butter and oil. Add the rice and stir to coat the kernels with
oil. Then add the water and remaining ingredients. Bring to boil,
then cover, reduce heat, and let simmer until all the water is absorbed,
about 5 minutes.

Fluff the rice with a fork and remove the cinnamon stick and lime leaves.
Let cool.

For Cauliflower Mixture:

1 small white onion, diced

1 tbsp garlic, chopped

1 tbsp fresh ginger, chopped

2 tbsp unsalted butter

1 tbsp yellow mustard seed, toasted and ground

1 tbsp coriander seed, toasted and ground

3 pods green cardamom seeds, toasted and ground

2 tbsp Madras curry powder

¼ tsp asafetida powder

1 tsp salt

1 tsp white pepper

4 cups cauliflower (about 1 small head), chopped

1 can coconut milk

1 whole egg

1 cup sliced almonds, toasted

¼ cup green onions, sliced

Preheat oven to 375°F.

In a large, heavy-bottomed pan, sauté onions, garlic, and ginger in butter. Add toasted seeds, powders, salt, and pepper, and lightly sauté to let the spices release their oils. Then add cauliflower and coconut milk. Cook slowly, stirring occasionally until cauliflower is just soft. Add rice to cauliflower mixture and stir in the egg, toasted almonds, and green onions.

Press mixture into a buttered and parchment-lined square cake pan or individual ramekins and bake in oven until firm, about 30 minutes.

To Plate: Place tuna on warm rice pudding cake. Drizzle sauce over top and stand watercress salad on top of tuna.

Serves 4

Beverage Pairing: **Malvasia**

Scorched Tuna with Sweet Mirin and Miso Sauce, Black Thai Rice and Shitake Mushroom Patties, and Braised Gai Lan

Scorched Tuna With Sweet Mirin and Miso Sauce

¼ cup white wine

¼ cup mirin

½ litre water

1 lemon, halved

1 orange, halved

pinch chile flakes

pinch togarashi

dash soy sauce

1 tsp ground Szechuan peppercorns

½ tsp coriander seeds

1 tsp bonito flakes

2 tbsp shiro miso

1 lb fresh Ahi or Albacore tuna, cut into 4 equal portions

In a large saucepan, combine all ingredients except shiro miso and tuna, and bring to a boil for 5 minutes. Remove orange and lemon halves. Reduce remaining liquid by ½.

Strain the sauce. Return sauce to heat, stir in shiro miso and reduce until sauce is shiny, translucent, and almost syrupy. Set aside.

Reserve tuna for plating, when it will be "scorched" by sauce.

Black Thai Rice and Shitake Mushroom Patties, and Braised Gai Lan

1 cup black Thai rice

2 cups water (or 1 16-oz can coconut milk)

¼ cup panko

¼ cup shitake mushrooms, sautéed

1 egg

4 green onion tops, chopped

zest of 1 lemon, finely chopped

1 tsp olive oil

1 sprig fresh cilantro

dash sesame oil

salt and pepper to taste

1 bunch gai lan, ends trimmed

¼ cup mirin

2 tbsp shiro miso

2 sheets nori, cut in half on the diagonal (for plating)

flying fish roe or caviar (garnish)

black sesame seeds (garnish)

Preheat oven to 350°F.

In a covered stockpot on medium heat, cook rice in water or milk for 40 minutes. Remove from heat and let sit for 10 minutes before transferring to a bowl.

When rice has cooled, add panko, sautéed shitake mushrooms, egg, green onions, lemon zest, olive oil, cilantro, sesame oil, salt, and pepper. Using your hands, mix well and form into 4 equal patties.

In a saucepan, heat olive oil. Fry patties for one minute each side. Transfer to a baking dish and heat in oven for 10 minutes.

In the meantime, in a saucepan over high heat, braise gai lan in miso and mirin sauce. Remove gai lan.

The sauce can be made a day ahead and brought back to a boil before serving.

To Plate: Slice raw tuna into ¼-inch thickness, about 4-5 slices per person. Put a rice cake in the centre of a soup bowl. Place slices of tuna on the side of rice cake and gai lan on tuna. Lightly spoon boiling sauce over tuna until outer surface is scorched. Lightly toast nori triangles until soft and pliable. Form each into cone, and stand on top of tuna. Garnish with flying fish roe or caviar and black sesame seeds.

Serves 4

Beverage Pairing: **Sylvaner**

Duck Three Ways: Silk Road Confit/Spring Rolls/Rice Noodle Salad

Silk Road Confit

2 tbsp kosher salt

¼ cup fresh ginger, sliced

8 whole garlic cloves, peeled

10 Kaffir lime leaves

2 cinnamon sticks

2 oranges, sliced

1 red onion, sliced

1 stalk fresh lemongrass, chopped

8 duck pieces (legs and thighs)

1 tbsp Chinese five-spice powder

1 tbsp ground Szechuan pepper

rendered duck fat, enough to cover meat

In a large mixing bowl, combine salt, ginger, garlic, lime leaves, cinammon, oranges, onion, and lemongrass. Cover duck pieces with marinade. Place a plate on top, weighed down with a smaller bowl, and leave in fridge overnight.

The next day, preheat oven to 350°F.

Remove the duck legs from the marinade and pat dry.

In a heavy-bottomed roasting pan on medium heat, brown the duck. Sprinkle the five-spice powder and Szechuan pepper over the legs, then place reserved marinade over the legs and cover with the duck fat. Cover and braise in the oven until meat is very tender, about 1-1½ hours.

Remove from the fat and let cool. Shred meat.

Return the other 4 legs to the oven to crisp the skin, about 20 minutes. Reserve for salad and spring rolls.

Green Tea Lychee Syrup

6 basil leaves

1 tsp mirin

1 cup lychee syrup

2 cups water

3 bags green tea

½ tsp salt

½ tsp ground white pepper

2 tbsp white sugar

dash soy sauce

1 whole green cardamom

1 tsp ground coriander

½ stick lemongrass, crushed

1 tbsp butter

Using a food processor, blend basil leaves with mirin. In a saucepan, combine leaves and mirin with remaining ingredients except butter and simmer for 20 minutes. Strain sauce and reduce to desired strength. *Monte au beurre* (mount with butter) to finish sauce, adding shine and smoothing flavour.

Spring Rolls

2 cups shitake mushrooms, sliced

1 tbsp olive oil

1 tbsp chopped garlic

1 tbsp chopped fresh ginger

zest of 1 small orange

2 confit duck legs, skinned and shredded (see page 110)

2 medium white onions, sliced and caramelized

salt and pepper to taste

1 tsp sesame oil

4 sheets spring roll wrappers

vegetable oil for deep-frying

In a saucepan on medium heat, sauté mushrooms in oil until tender. Add garlic, ginger, orange zest, duck meat, and onions. Add salt and pepper to taste, then drizzle with sesame oil. Let cool. Stuff spring rolls as per instructions on the package.

In a deep-fat fryer at 350°F, deep-fry rolls until golden.

Makes 4.

Rice Noodle Salad

½ cup ponzu sauce (see sidebar)

1 cup papaya, julienned

2 bundles rice noodles, blanched

2 confit duck legs, skinned and shredded (see page 110)

2 tbsp fresh cilantro, chopped

1 green onion, finely chopped

To make ponzu sauce, combine ¼ cup freshly squeezed orange juice, ¼ cup soy sauce and 1 tbsp sesame oil.

In a saucepan over medium heat, warm ponzu sauce. In a large bowl, toss together papaya, noodles, green onions, cilantro, ponzu sauce, and duck meat.

To Plate: On a rectangular Asian-style plate, line up the three dishes in a row: spring roll (cut in ½) at one end, salad at the other, and the duck with syrup in the middle.

Serves 4

Beverage Pairing: **Sancerre or Sake**

Grilled Chinese Pepper-Crusted Venison, Water Chestnuts and Shitake Mushroom Sauce, Yam with Mascarpone and Chive *Gâteaux*, Fresh Mango or Papaya Salad

Yam with Mascarpone and Chive *Gâteaux*

2 large yams, peeled and thinly sliced with a mandoline

¾ cup mascarpone cheese

1 bunch chives, finely chopped

salt and pepper to taste

Using a small, round cookie cutter, cut yam slices into circles, at least 8 to 10 circles per ramekin.

Preheat oven to 350°F.

In a food processor, blend chives and mascarpone. Season to taste. Using 4 greased ramekins, begin with 2 slices of yam, then a layer mascarpone chive mixture. Continue layering in this way until ramekins are full. Cook in a *bain-marie* (see page 21) covered with foil, until yam is tender, about ½ hour.

Grilled Chinese Pepper-Crusted Venison

4 4-oz venison tenderloin pieces

1 tbsp Chinese five-spice powder

1 tbsp freshly ground Szechuan peppercorns

 salt and white pepper to taste

Preheat oven to 350°F.

Season venison with five-spice powder, peppercorns, salt, and pepper. Mark each side with a cross-hatch pattern. Roast in oven or on indoor grill pan 5 minutes for medium-rare, 8 minutes for medium. Let meat rest before slicing.

Water Chestnuts and Shitake Mushroom Sauce

1 cup shitake mushrooms, sliced

½ can water chestnuts, sliced

1 clove garlic, chopped

2 tbsp butter

1 cup veal demi-glace (see page 17)

1 tbsp butter (to finish)

In a saucepan over medium heat, sauté mushrooms, water chestnuts, and garlic in butter. Add demi-glace and finish with butter.

Fresh Mango or Papaya Salad

1 ripe mango or papaya, peeled, seeded and cut into large cubes

1 jalapeño pepper, seeds in, finely diced (see page 16)

juice of 2 limes

½ red onion, finely diced

1 bunch fresh cilantro, chopped

salt and white pepper to taste

In a large serving bowl, mix all ingredients. Place in fridge for 4 hours before serving to let flavours combine.

To Plate: Remove *gâteaux* from ramekins and place one on each plate. Pour sauce on top. Cut venison into thin slices and place on top of *gâteau*. Arrange salad around *gâteau*. Drizzle plate with truffle oil.

Serves 4

Beverage Pairing: **Riposso Valpolicella**

Tiramisu Free-Style Won Ton Stack with Caramelized and Rum Coffee Sauce

Tiramisu Free-Style Won Ton Stack

1 cup whipping cream

1 cup shaved Belgium chocolate

2 egg yolks

6 tbsp sugar

½ tsp vanilla extract

1⅛ cup Marsala wine

8 oz mascarpone cheese (room temperature)

1¼ cup whipping cream

1 tsp icing sugar

6 wontons per serving, fried according to directions on package

In a double boiler over low heat, combine whipping cream and shaved chocolate. When chocolate has melted, remove from heat and set aside.

Using a hand mixer, cream together the egg yolks and sugar until the mixture is smooth and pale yellow in colour. Add vanilla extract and wine and whisk. Add mascarpone in small quantities and whisk until incorporated and the mixture is fluffy and smooth.

In a separate bowl, with clean beaters, whip cream with icing sugar until soft peaks form. Add the mascarpone mixture and whisk until stiff peaks form.

Caramelized Rum and Coffee Sauce

⅛ cup sugar

¼ cup dark rum

¼ cup brewed strong coffee or espresso

¼ cup whipping cream

In a saucepan on medium heat, caramelize sugar. Add rum and burn off alcohol. Add coffee and cream and reduce, stirring occasionally until the sugar has been absorbed and the sauce is thick enough to adhere to a plate.

To Plate: Assemble wontons and pour sauce over top.

Serves 4

Beverage Pairing: **Ruby Port**

Holiday Party

Classic Mussels or *Moules Marinière*

3 garlic cloves, minced

2 tbsp extra-virgin olive oil

10 cherry tomatoes, halved

1 pinch red chile flakes

1 lb fresh mussels, bearded, rinsed and cleaned (see page 23)

½ cup dry white wine

⅛ cup unsalted butter

1 pinch *herbes de Provence*

freshly ground black pepper to taste

In a large skillet with a lid, on medium heat, lightly sauté garlic in olive oil. Add tomatoes and when they have just started to release their liquid, add chile flakes and mussels and simmer for 30 seconds. Add white wine, butter, herbs, and pepper, cover and let steam until all mussels have cooked, about 3-5 minutes. Discard any unopened mussels.

To Plate: Serve with warm bread of your choice for dipping in the broth or go all the way and make *pommes frites* or French fries, the classic Belgian preparation, also served with garlic mayonnaise or aioli (see page 50) for dipping the fries.

Serves 4

Beverage Pairing: **Belgian Style Red or Amber Ale**

Spinach Salad, Wild Mushroom Sauté with Mascarpone Dressing

1 lb mixed mushrooms of your choice

¼ tsp olive oil

1 lb spinach

¼ cup white wine vinegar

3 tbsp pink peppercorns

2 cups mascarpone cheese

salt and white pepper to taste

In a saucepan on medium heat, sauté mushrooms in olive oil until they cook down to ⅓ original volume, about 3 minutes. Add spinach to wilt lightly. Remove spinach and transfer to a serving bowl or dish.

In a separate mixing bowl, whisk together white wine vinegar, pink peppercorns, and mascarpone. Season with salt and white pepper.

Warm dressing in the same pan that you cooked the mushrooms in.

To Plate: Place warm spinach and mushroom mixture into ring mould. Pour a little dressing over salad to coat lightly and hold it together. Around base of ring, pour a little more dressing as garnish. Remove mould from salad, which should now stand up nicely. Garnish top of salad with long, sesame-seed bread stick or your favourite croutons.

Serves 4

Beverage Pairing: **Fumé Blanc**

Wild Mushroom Reggiano Risotto with Truffle Oil Drizzle and Portobello Chips

Portobello Chips

2 large portobello mushroom caps, thinly sliced

vegetable oil for deep-frying

salt and pepper to taste

Using a deep-fat fryer, heat enough vegetable oil to cover mushrooms to 350°F. Fry portobello slices until crispy. Drain on paper towel and season with salt and black pepper.

Wild Mushroom Reggiano Risotto with Truffle Oil Drizzle

3 cups assorted fresh wild mushrooms
   (morels, chanterelles, porcini, or hedgehogs), sliced

2 tbsp unsalted butter

2 tbsp olive oil

3 tbsp unsalted butter

4 tbsp olive oil

4 small shallots, minced

2 cups arborio rice

½ cup dry white wine

8-10 cups low-sodium chicken stock, heated

¼ cup reduced veal stock (see page 17)

½ cup freshly grated Parmesan cheese

salt and pepper to taste

4 tsp truffle oil (to finish)

shaved Parmesan cheese (garnish)

fresh chives, whole or chopped (garnish)

In a saucepan on medium heat, sauté wild mushrooms in 2 tbsp butter and 2 tbsp olive oil. Set aside.

In another saucepan, melt 2 tbsp butter and 4 tbsp olive oil. Sweat the shallots about 4 minutes. Add the rice and stir until just coated with the butter and olive oil. Add the white wine. Slowly add the chicken stock, 2 cups at a time, stirring continuously until rice is creamy and *al dente*. Add the reduced veal stock and sautéed wild mushrooms.

Remove from heat. Add the grated Parmesan and the remaining 1 tbsp butter. Stir to combine all of the ingredients. The texture should be creamy, but not soupy. Season with salt and pepper to taste.

To Plate: Divide rice into 4 serving bowls and drizzle each with 1 tsp truffle oil. Place mushroom chips on top and garnish with shaved Parmesan and fresh chives. Serve piping hot.

Serves 4

Beverage Pairing: California Syrah

Turkey Osso Buco with Oven-Dried Cranberry Sauce, Maple-Roasted Yam Biscuits, Buckwheat Honey-Glazed Brussels Sprouts, and Cinnamon-Dusted Carrots

Turkey Osso Buco with Oven-Dried Cranberry Sauce

¼ lb fresh cranberries, for oven-drying (see side bar)

8 turkey drumsticks, thick end cut by your butcher into 3-inch thick rounds

flour seasoned with salt and pepper, for dredging

¼ cup butter

1 large white onion

2 carrots

3 celery stocks

2 bay leaves

3 sage leaves

6 whole dried allspice berries

9 whole black peppercorns

10 whole garlic cloves, peeled

1 tbsp tomato paste

½ litre dry white wine

water to cover

¼ cup butter

salt and pepper to taste

To oven-dry cranberries, place on a baking tray lined with parchment paper and bake in a 150°F. oven for about 5 hours.

Preheat oven to 350°F.

Dredge turkey rounds in seasoned flour. In a hot skillet, melt butter and lightly brown turkey rounds.

In a large casserole dish or roasting pan, combine all ingredients except cranberries, butter, salt, and pepper. Cover with water and roast in oven until well done or turkey pulls easily away from the bone, approximately 3 hours. If the liquid starts to evaporate too quickly, add more water and wine (2 parts water to 1 part wine). Remove turkey rounds and set aside.

In a saucepan over medium heat, reduce liquid by ½ to ⅔ until approximately ½ litre remains. Strain stock, add oven-dried cranberries, butter, salt, and pepper.

Maple-Roasted Yam Biscuits

1 medium yam, chopped into 1-inch cubes

⅛ cup maple syrup

salt and white pepper to taste

3 tbsp unsalted butter

Preheat oven to 325°F.

In a bowl, combine yam, maple syrup, salt, and pepper. Line a cookie sheet with parchment paper and spread yam mixture evenly.

Cut butter into small cubes and toss onto the yams. Bake in oven until yams are soft. Cool and set aside.

2 cups flour

2 tsp sugar

1 tsp baking soda

½ tsp salt

¼ cup shortening

2 tbsp currants

¾ cup buttermilk

1 tsp cream of tartar

Preheat oven to 425°F. Grease and flour a baking sheet.

In a large bowl, sift together the flour, sugar, baking soda, and salt. With your fingers or 2 knives, work in the shortening until the mixture resembles coarse crumbs. Stir in the roasted yams and make a well in the centre of the mix. Stir cream of tartar into the buttermilk and add to the well. Stir lightly, until the dough clings together. It should be soft and sticky, so add more liquid if necessary.

On a floured board, knead dough lightly for 1 minute. Pat it out to 1-inch thickness.

With a 1½-inch pastry or cookie cutter, stamp out rounds. Transfer rounds to baking sheet and bake in the oven until lightly browned and skewer inserted in middle comes out clean, about 15 minutes.

Makes 6-8 biscuits.

Buckwheat Honey-Glazed Brussels Sprouts

12 Brussels sprouts

2 tbsp buckwheat honey

With a knife, make an X in core of each sprout. In a pot of water, blanch sprouts until just soft. Add honey and mix.

Cinnamon-Dusted Carrots

12 baby carrots

⅛ tsp ground cinnamon

½ tsp sugar

3 tbsp water or stock

salt and pepper to taste

1 tbsp butter

In a pot of water, blanch carrots. In a pan on high heat, combine blanched carrots and remaining ingredients until water has evaporated and carrots are shiny and glazed. Serve at once.

To Plate: Because this is a rustic dish, it needs less plate fondling. Place turkey rounds on plate, cover with generous amount of sauce, and serve with the yam biscuits, Brussels sprouts, and carrots.

Serves 4

Beverage Pairing: **Gamay Noir**

Citrus and Five-Spice Duck Confit, Shaved Fennel, Orange and Candy-Striped Beet Salad with Pomegranate Dressing, and 5-Tribe Celebration Bread

A classic old-world French preparation, *confit* means to preserve. This dish was invented before refrigeration. Storing duck in its own fat made it non-permeable by air, and thus non-perishable. You can buy duck fat in tubs, which should be readily available from your local butcher. The fat will cook off when reheated so the duck won't be greasy; it will be tender and very flavourful. Here, we add a modern spice treatment that makes the dish suitable for any time of year. Another confit recipe appears on page 110.

Citrus and Five-Spice Duck Confit

4 large duck legs and thighs

2 tbsp coarse kosher salt

enough duck fat to render (available from your butcher)

1 tbsp Chinese five-spice powder

1 tbsp freshly ground black pepper

1 tbsp Szechuan pepper

1 tbsp salt

1 cinnamon stick

6 cloves garlic, peeled

4 whole star anise

1 red onion, sliced

1 fennel bulb, sliced

zest of 1 orange

same orange, quartered

zest of 1 lemon

same lemon, quartered

In a large bowl, season duck pieces with salt. Place a weight on top and refrigerate overnight. The next day, drain duck and pat pieces dry.

Preheat oven to 400°F.

In a large saucepan on medium heat, sauté pieces in duck fat until golden brown, about 7 minutes.

In a large baking dish or roaster, mix duck with remaining ingredients. Cover with duck fat and foil and bake in oven until the meat is extremely tender, about 1½ hours.

Remove legs from fat. Strain fat and discard other ingredients.

Pour the duck fat back onto the meat and let cool. When completely cooled, cover and refrigerate overnight.

When ready to serve, remove legs from fat and reheat in a 400°F oven until skin is crispy, about 20 minutes. Reserve some fat for bread (see page 127).

Shaved Fennel, Blood Orange, and Candy-Striped Beet Salad with Pomegranate Dressing

2 bulbs fennel, finely shaved

4 blood oranges, seeded and segmented

½ cup pomegranate seeds

8 small candy-striped beets, blanched until fork tender, peeled and diced

¼ cup pomegranate molasses

1½ oz honey

1 oz white wine vinegar

1 tbsp Dijon mustard

1 tsp salt

1 tsp ground white pepper

½ cup vegetable oil

In a large bowl, combine fennel, oranges, beets, and seeds.

In a food processor or blender, combine remaining ingredients, except vegetable oil. Slowly add oil and blend until emulsified.

Add enough dressing to fennel mixture to coat.

5-Tribe Celebration Bread

1¼ cups flour

1¼ cups cornmeal

1¼ tsp baking powder

3 cups cream

2 eggs

2 tbsp melted butter

1 lb yam, blanched and cubed into raisin-sized pieces

½ cup dried apricots

½ cup dried cranberries

½ cup fresh thyme

Preheat oven to 350°F.

In a bowl, mix flour, cornmeal, and baking powder.

In a separate bowl, blend cream, eggs, and butter. Add yams, fruit, and thyme.

Add dry ingredients to wet and blend but do not over mix. Batter should be easy to pour, but not runny.

Pour batter into muffin tins greased with the duck fat and bake until center is moist, about 20-30 minutes or until wooden skewer inserted into centre of muffins comes out clean.

To Plate: Arrange the salad in the centre of the plate and place a duck leg or thigh leaning on one side. Slice bread on the bias and trim the ends to stand on plate. Drizzle with extra dressing and garnish with fennel fronds.

Serves 4

Beverage Pairing: Alsacian Gewürztraminer or Full-bodied Pinôt Noir

Grilled Pasture-Grazed New Zealand Venison, Stilton, Caramelized Onion and Buttermilk Waffle, Black Velvet Sauce

The luxurious melding of Cassis, Guinness beer, and chocolate is a gastronomic version of black velvet, and works exquisitely with venison.

Grilled Venison

4 4-oz venison tenderloins steaks, centre cut

salt and pepper to taste

Preheat oven to 350°F.

Season venison with salt and pepper. In a pan on high heat, sear venison until lightly caramelized (a browned crust), about 1 minute each side. Sear ends as well to seal in the juice. Roast in oven to medium or medium-rare (preferred), about 7 minutes. Remove and let rest before slicing.

When searing meat, do not move it in the pan; simply keep it in place. When meat is properly seared, it will lift easily, not stick and tear. And remember, the pan must be smokin'!!

Black Velvet Sauce

2 cups veal demi-glace (see page 17)

2 cups Guinness beer

2 shallots, chopped

2 whole black peppercorns

1 whole allspice berry

1 whole juniper berry

2 tbsp Ribena

2 tbsp Crème de Cassis

2 tbsp unsweetened dark chocolate

In a large saucepan over medium heat, combine all ingredients and reduce by ⅓. Set aside.

Stilton, Caramelized Onion and Buttermilk Waffle

2 yellow onions, thinly sliced

2 tbsp butter

1 sprig fresh thyme

½ cup port wine

2 cups all-purpose flour

4 tsp baking powder

1 tsp baking soda

¼ tsp salt

2 whole eggs

2 cups buttermilk

salt and pepper to taste

pinch of garlic salt

pinch nutmeg

½ cup Stilton cheese, crumbled

6 tbsp clarified butter (see page 21)

2 bunches wilted spinach (see sidebar) (for plating)

3 tbsp butter (to finish)

To wilt spinach, melt butter with a dash of nutmeg and pinch of garlic. Add spinach (leaves only) and sweat until garlic is cooked.

In a saucepan on medium heat, caramelize onions in butter, stirring constantly until they are golden brown. Add thyme and deglaze with port and cook until all the liquid is absorbed. Remove from heat and let cool.

In a large mixing bowl, combine the flour, baking powder and soda, and salt. In a separate bowl, combine the eggs, buttermilk, salt, pepper, garlic salt, and nutmeg. Incorporate dry ingredients into wet to form a batter. If the mixture is too dry, add a touch of milk. If it is too wet, add a touch of flour. Stir in crumbled Stilton and caramelized onion. Season with salt and pepper.

Brush waffle maker with clarified butter. Drop in batter.

To Plate: Place wilted spinach in the centre of a large plate. Fan venison slices on each side. Cut waffle into 4 and stack on one side. Spoon reheated sauce over top and *monte au beurre* (mount with butter).

Serves 4

Beverage Pairing: Cabernet Sauvignon

Grilled Lamb Sirloin with Candied Shallots, Wild Mushroom Savory Honey Baklava, and Roast Garlic and Lemon Baby Carrots

Grilled Lamb Sirloin

4 4-6-oz lamb sirloin steaks

¼ cup olive oil

4 shallots, sliced

zest and juice of 1 orange

1 tbsp fresh thyme, chopped

kosher salt and black pepper to taste

In a large pan, mix all ingredients and marinate lamb, covered in fridge, for 24 hours.

The next day, grill lamb until medium-rare: 2½-3 minutes per side for 4 oz lamb and 3-3½ minutes per side for 6 oz. Let rest before slicing.

Candied Shallots

2 tbsp olive oil

1 cup shallots

¼ cup white sugar

¼ cup chicken stock (see page 18)

⅛ cup balsamic vinegar

salt and pepper to taste

2 cups Cabernet

½ cup chicken stock

2 cups veal stock (see page 17)

¼ cup cold butter, diced

Preheat oven to 350°F.

To candy shallots: in a frying pan on high heat, heat olive oil. Add shallots and caramelize until nicely browned, about 3 minutes. Add sugar to pan and let caramelize some more until golden brown.

Add the ¼ cup chicken stock, balsamic vinegar, salt, and pepper. Cover and roast in oven for about 20 minutes, adding a little more stock if pan gets dry, until shallots are soft yet still hold their shape.

Remove from oven and glaze with a little of the sugar syrup.

In the meantime, in a saucepan on high heat, combine Cabernet, veal and chicken stock, and reduce by ⅔. Add candied shallots to warm through. Finish with cold butter.

Wild Mushroom Savory Honey Baklava

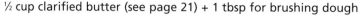

½ cup clarified butter (see page 21) + 1 tbsp for brushing dough

1 250-gram pkg mascarpone cheese

9 cups wild mushrooms (chanterelles, porcini, crimini), sliced

4 tbsp butter

salt and pepper to taste

1 tsp fresh rosemary, chopped

⅓ cup white wine

¼ cup pine nuts, toasted

3 tbsp truffle honey

⅛ cup Cinzano

1 pkg phyllo dough (see sidebar)

When working with phyllo, thaw in fridge overnight. Try to work quickly and keep reserved sheets covered with a damp kitchen towel. Butter between the layers to create flaky pastry.

In a large bowl, combine ½ cup clarified butter, and mascarpone cheese. Set aside.

In a saucepan on high heat, sauté mushrooms in butter, and season with salt and pepper. (Mushrooms love butter and will soak it up, so be liberal if you like.) Add rosemary and white wine and continue to sauté until they are brown and reduced to about ½ the original volume. Stir in toasted pine nuts.

Set aside and let cool. There should be no liquid left in pan when done.

To make glaze, gently heat Cinzano with truffle honey for about 2 minutes.

Preheat oven to 350°F.

In a rectangular, removeable-bottomed baking pan, assemble layers of phyllo dough, about 8 layers high. One layer is composed of 1 phyllo sheet, brushed with clarified butter and folded to fit pan, 2 tbsp mascarpone mix, spread out evenly, and ⅛ of mushroom mix. Top the last sheet with cracked black pepper and rosemary. Bake for ½ hour, drizzling glaze over top after 15 minutes.

Roast Garlic and Lemon Baby Carrots

12 baby carrots with green tops trimmed to 1 inch, peeled and blanched

¼ cup chicken stock (see page 18)

juice of 3 lemons

6 roasted garlic cloves, roughly chopped (see page 15)

salt and white pepper to taste

1 tbsp butter

½ bunch flat leaf (Italian) parsley, julienned

To blanch carrots, boil in salted water until *al dente*, about 5 minutes. Refresh under cold water. Set aside.

In a saucepan, bring chicken stock and lemon juice to boil. Add carrots, roasted garlic, and salt and pepper. Finish with butter and sprinkle with parsley.

To Plate: Place mushroom baklava on one side of plate. Pour 1 oz warm sauce next to it, along with a couple of whole shallots. Arrange sliced lamb on sauce without covering all of it. Stand carrots, green ends up, next to baklava, tucking the tips under edges of sliced lamb.

Serves 4

Beverage Pairing: **Australian Shiraz**

Old-Fashioned Bread and Butter Pudding with Rum and Raisin Sauce

2 eggs

1½ cups whipping cream

1⁄16 tsp freshly grated nutmeg

1 pinch ground cloves

1 pinch ground allspice

zest of 1 orange, finely chopped

½ cup granulated sugar

1 large baguette, crust trimmed, cut into ½-inch pieces

¼ cup butter, melted

1⁄16 tsp vanilla extract

If puddings have been made ahead of time, place them on a baking sheet lined with parchment paper and reheat in a 400°F oven for about 5 minutes. To make sure they are hot enough, insert a metal skewer into the pudding, remove and touch it to your lip. If it feels warm, the pudding is evenly cooked through.

In a large bowl, whisk together all ingredients except for bread, melted butter, and vanilla. Add bread cubes, mixing with hands. Set aside for 15 minutes.

Preheat oven to 350°F.

Butter 4 ramekins. Using your hands, squeeze excess moisture from bread cubes and pack into ramekins. Pour remainder of liquid equally over all 4. Melt butter, add vanilla and evenly distribute over all 4 ramekins. Bake in *bain-marie* (see page 21) for 1 hour. Set aside to cool.

Rum and Raisin Sauce

¼ cup granulated sugar

½ cup unsalted butter

¼ cup dark rum

¼ cup golden sultana raisins

In a saucepan on medium heat, caramelize sugar in butter until golden brown. Do not burn. Pour rum into saucepan and ignite to burn off alcohol. Bring rum to a boil, add raisins and butter, and stir until sauce is smooth and well mixed and pulls away from sides of the pan.

To Plate: Remove bread puddings form ramekins. Place in centre of plate and pour sauce over top.

Serves 6

Beverage Pairing: **B.C. Brandenburg #3/Warm Cognac**

Layered Amaretto-Scented Pound Cake, White Chocolate Mousse, and Lemon Curd

A bit of fun like your grandma used to have. Weigh the 12 eggs; this will also be the weight of the dry ingredients.

For Cake:

12 large eggs

12 eggs/weight: sugar

pinch of salt

12 eggs/weight: butter, melted and cooled

12 eggs/weight: flour

1 cup Amaretto

Preheat oven to 350°F.

Break eggs, keeping yolks separate from whites. Beat yolks, sugar, and salt until the mixture becomes white and creamy.

Beat in the melted butter. Add flour and Amaretto.

Whip the egg whites until stiff peaks form. Fold egg whites carefully into egg mixture.

Butter and flour a 10-inch-round cake pan.

Pour batter in all the way to the brim, wiping tins clean.

Bake in oven for 30 minutes or until a wooden skewer inserted in the middle comes out clean.

Lemon Curd:

100 grams unsalted butter

225 grams sugar

3 whole eggs

zest and juice of 6 large lemons

Using a double boiler, melt butter, then gradually add sugar, 3 beaten eggs, the lemon zest and juice, whisking constantly until it thickens, about 7-12 minutes.

For White Chocolate Mousse:

2 cups white chocolate, broken into small pieces

½ cup whipping cream + 3 cups whipping cream

Using a double boiler, combine chocolate with ½ cup whipping cream, whisking until everything is smooth and incorporated. Take off heat and let cool.

Whip the 3 cups whipping cream to form a thick cream and incorporate the melted white chocolate.

To Plate: Slice cake into 7 layers. Layer mousse and curd on each layer. Drizzle top of cake with Amaretto, a dollop of mousse, and top with fresh seasonal berries.

Serves 4

Beverage Pairing: Moscato d'Asti

Wild Sockeye Salmon in Cedar
Sheath and Cedar Gelée Glazed Baby
Vegetables with Apricot Fig Riesling
Nectar (page 60).

Cold-Smoked Halibut Brandade (page 34)
and 3-Citrus Halibut Ceviche (page 70).

Beef Wellington and Roast Garlic
Chive Mash Potatoes (page 181).

Fresh clipped Greens (page 170).

Scallop and Tiger Prawn Tournedos with
Bonito Butter Sauce, Tobiko, Leek Tempura,
and Cucumber Salsa (page 29).

Sevruga Caviar and Crème Fraiche Stuffed Nugget Potatoes (page 39), Ancho Chile-Dusted and Fragrant Lime Beef Tenderloin Pickup Sticks (page 35), 3-Chile Marinated Sweet Potato-Wrapped Prawns (page 27), Crispy Risotto Balls with Gooey Cheese Centres (page 36), Oven-Dried Tomato and Goat Cheese Salsa (page 37), and Grilled Asparagus (page 42).

Erotic Chocolate Fondue and
Dipping Goodies (page 183).

New Traditional Dinner Party

Original Tijuana Caesar Salad with Classic Dressing and Lemon Pepper-Grilled Crouton

Caesar salad was invented in Tijuana, Mexico but made famous in New York. Essentially, the salad is all about the dressing, so all the flavours should be strong and discernable, not like the "mayonnaisesque" ones we've grown accustomed to. The dressing should not be served "goopy"; it should coat and cling to each leaf of Romaine and yet not coat the plate when the salad is finished.

Try a toasted long slice of baguette or focaccia as a crouton rather than those ridiculous little bread cubes. And adding chicken or shrimp is a profit enhancer invented for restaurants, not a flavour enhancer. This is a stand-alone salad!

6 cloves garlic, peeled

10 anchovy fillets

2 tbsp capers, drained

1 tbsp ground black pepper to taste

1 tsp coarse salt

2 tbsp Worcestershire sauce

juice of 2 lemons

2 large eggs, yolks only

1 heaping tbsp Dijon mustard

⅓ cup + extra for garnish Parmesan cheese, freshly grated

1 tsp Louisiana hot sauce

3 cups good quality, neutral-flavoured mayonnaise

½ cup extra-virgin olive oil

2 large heads Romaine lettuce leaves, washed and spun dry

juice of 1 lemon

3 or 4 pieces of focaccia (or your favourite bread)

¼ cup melted butter

zest of 1 lemon, chopped

1 tbsp ground black pepper

This recipe makes more than enough for 4 portions so dress the salad according to the instructions, unless you want to do it the classic French way and make individual bowls tableside *à la minute* dressing. It's easier to get the flavour components right by making a larger batch, and the leftover dressing keeps nicely in the fridge for 2 weeks.

In a food processor, purée garlic, anchovies, capers, pepper, salt, egg yolks, lemon juice, and Worcestershire sauce. Add mustard, Parmesan cheese, hot sauce, and mayonnaise and purée again. Finish with extra-virgin olive oil and black pepper, drizzling oil in slowly with processor running.

Toss with torn or whole leaf Romaine. Sprinkle with lemon juice and garnish with Parmesan.

Brush bread with melted butter and sprinkle with chopped lemon zest and pepper. Toast in a 350°F oven for about 7 minutes.

Serves 4

Beverage Pairing: **Pinôt Blanc**

Smoked Roma Tomatoes with Andouille Sausage and Mussels

1 large Andouille or chorizo sausage, chopped

2 tbsp extra-virgin olive oil

5 smoked Roma tomatoes, chopped (see page 24)

1 tbsp garlic, chopped

1 lb fresh mussels, bearded, rinsed, and cleaned (see page 23)

½ cup dry white wine

⅛ cup unsalted butter

1 pinch saffron

ground black pepper to taste

In a large skillet with a lid, on medium heat, lightly sauté sausage in olive oil until its natural oil begins to release. Add garlic, tomatoes, and mussels and cook on high heat for 30 seconds. Stir in white wine, butter, saffron, and pepper. Cover and let steam until all mussels have opened, about 3-5 minutes. Discard any unopened mussels.

Serves 1 as an entrée or 4 as an appetizer

Beverage Pairing: Cabernet Franc

Foil Poached Sole with Mixed Vegetables

Okay! Here's one for the bachelors and bachelorettes. No clean-up required for this classic French preparation of fish. I chose sole because it cooks quickly and has a delicate, buttery flavour with juices that combine with the other ingredients to create a full entrée in one simple parcel. This leaves more time to get onto the matter at hand: not remaining a bachelor or bachelorette. Wows 'em every time.

4 8" x 11" pieces tinfoil or cooking parchment paper

1 large leek, white part only, chopped

1 large fennel bulb, chopped

1 bunch spring green beans, chopped

1 large sweet bell pepper, julienned

1 cup seasonal mushrooms, chopped

1 cup patty pan squash (or your favourite winter squash)

8 sprigs fresh thyme, chopped

4 fresh Dover sole fillets (or your local sole)

2 cups white wine

½ cup unsalted butter

sea salt and white pepper to taste

Preheat oven to 350°F.

Fold foil or parchment in half, crimping both sides to form a pouch.

Mix vegetables and thyme and separate into four equal portions.

Place one fillet in each pouch. Add vegetable mix, butter, and wine in equal portions to the pouches. Season with sea salt and white pepper.

Seal top of each pouch, making sure there are several folds in all the seams so that the liquid will not leak out. Place pouches flat on a baking sheet and cook until fish lightly flakes but is still moist, about 10 minutes.

To Plate: Place unopened parcel on the plate. Slice open with knife and pull edges apart. The aromatic steam will waft out, creating a mouthwatering sensation!

Serves 4

Beverage Pairing: Dry Riesling

Pan-Seared Wild Sockeye Salmon with Candied Shallot Beaujolais Reduction, Wild Rice Waffles, and Fresh Clipped Greens

When in season, fresh wild sockeye salmon is a delicacy. Lightly seasoned, with its crispy skin and rich fatty flesh, this fish oozes sensuality. The perfect combination of the young fruity wine and candied shallots complement both the salmon and the savory waffle. The other great thing about the waffles is that they can be prepared the day before the party, leaving you time to concentrate on the salmon and sauce. The simplicity of preparation understates the complex flavours and will win over your guests, leading them to proclaim that the closet gourmet has now, finally, come out.

Wild Rice Waffles

2 whole eggs
1 cup 2% milk
1 cup cooked wild rice (see page 16)
⅛ cup fresh chives, chopped
zest of 1 lemon
1 cup all-purpose flour
1 tsp baking powder
¼ tsp ground cardamom
½ tsp freshly ground coffee
salt and black pepper to taste

In a large bowl, whisk together eggs, milk, cooked wild rice, and chives. In a separate bowl, combine dry ingredients. Add to wet and blend to make a pancake-like batter. If the mixture is too dry, add a touch of milk. If it is too wet, add a touch of flour. Lightly butter a waffle iron and drop in batter. When waffles are ready, set aside. They can be rewarmed in the oven while salmon is cooking.

Candied Shallot Beaujolais Reduction

12 shallots, peeled

2 tbsp extra-virgin olive oil

¼ cup white sugar

½ cup chicken stock

1 cup Beaujolais wine

1 cinnamon stick

1 bay leaf

1 sprig fresh thyme

 salt and pepper to taste

In a lightly oiled hot skillet, sauté shallots in olive oil until they are golden brown. Sprinkle sugar in bottom of pan and let caramelize until the sugar becomes golden brown to brown, about 4 minutes. (Do not burn!) Add chicken stock, wine, cinnamon stick, bay leaf, thyme, and salt and pepper. Reduce heat to medium and simmer until liquid and sugar become syrup-like and the shallots are coated and soft throughout, about 15 minutes. If shallots are not soft by the time the liquid has reduced, add equal parts of chicken stock and wine until they soften. Add fresh thyme just before serving.

Pan-Seared Wild Sockeye Salmon

4 6-oz sockeye salmon fillets

1 tbsp extra-virgin olive oil

black pepper to taste

sea salt to taste

Preheat oven to 400°F.

Lightly oil salmon fillets. Season with sea salt and pepper. In an ovenproof skillet on high heat, sear salmon fillets until lightly browned, about 2 minutes each side. Roast in oven for 5 minutes until fillets are medium-rare.

Fresh Clipped Greens

Choose favorite seasonal greens other than lettuce, such as, nasturtiums, tat soi, mizuna, arugula, fresh sweet pea tips, and herbs.

2 cups seasonal greens
1 tbsp fresh lemon juice
2 tbsp Meyer lemon oil
¼ tsp sea salt
¼ tsp ground white pepper

In a large bowl, combine all ingredients and mix well.

To Plate: Place waffle on plate and set salmon on top. Arrange greens on top. Try to keep the greens "fluffy" and not squashed down. Drizzle salmon and plate with reduction, scattering shallots.

Serves 4

Beverage Pairing: **Gamay Noir**

Chermoula-Crusted Ostrich, Café au Lait Sauce and Medjool Date and Toasted Almond Saffron Pilaf

Chermoula-Crusted Ostrich

¼ tsp chile powder

¼ tsp cloves

¼ tsp cumin

¼ tsp coriander

¼ tsp allspice

¼ tsp cardamom

¼ tsp paprika

¼ tsp cayenne pepper

1 cup mint

1 cup parsley

3 cups lemon juice

1½ litre olive oil

¼ cup honey

zest of 2 limes

zest of 2 oranges

4 5-oz ostrich fans, or coins

Combine seasonings with lemon juice, olive oil, honey, and zests to form a loose paste.

Marinate ostrich in chermoula paste for 1 hour.

In a skillet over high heat, grill until medium-rare, about 3 minutes each side. Let rest before slicing.

Café au Lait Sauce

1 shot of espresso

1 cup Amaretto di Sarono liqueur

⅛ cup tamarind paste

⅛ cup heavy cream

½ cup veal demi-glace (see page 17)

In a saucepan over medium-high heat, combine all ingredients and reduce to ⅓. Transfer to blender to get sauce a little frothy just before serving.

Medjool Date and Toasted Almond Saffron Pilaf

1 medium yellow onion, finely chopped

1 tbsp butter

2 cups basmati rice

2 bay leaves

2 grams saffron

3 cups chicken stock (see page 18)

½ cup Medjool dates, chopped

½ cup toasted almonds

⅛ cup flat leaf (Italian) parsley, chopped

⅛ cup chives, chopped

In a saucepan on medium heat, sweat onions in butter. Add basmati rice and sweat another 2 minutes. Add bay leaves, saffron, chicken stock, and simmer over very low heat, covered, for about 25-30 minutes.

Add chopped dates and mix in with rice. Mix in almonds and chopped herbs.

To Plate: Slice ostrich and fan out pieces next to loose pile of pilaf (about 1 cup each serving). You can mould rice in a ring mould for a cleaner look. Pool sauce over ostrich.

Serves 4

Beverage Pairing: Sangiovese

Pan-Seared Organic Duck Breast with Bombay Mustard Sauce and Potato Salad

This dish uses 3 elements I love to work with: duck, curry, and potato salad. Duck, properly cooked – medium-rare with a crispy skin – is one of my all-time favourites. The warm potato salad will instantly win you over, as the creamy, and slightly tart cheese, nestles over the crispy potatoes with fresh peppery greens and smoky bacon. The addition of the fruited curry dressing takes the complex sauce issue away and makes this a diverse palate overachiever. This is my version of global warming at its best.

¼ cup grainy pomery mustard

1 tbsp curry powder or garam masala

1 ripe mango, peeled, pitted and sliced

splash of fruity white wine (like a Riesling)

4 medium-sized duck breasts

sea salt to taste

black pepper to taste

1 tbsp canola oil

nasturtium flowers or your favourite summer greens (garnish)

pistachio oil (optional) (to finish)

In a blender, purée mustard, curry powder or garam masala, white wine, and mango slices until smooth. Salt and pepper to taste and place in a squirt bottle.

Preheat oven to 350°F.

Prepare duck by using a sharp knife to make a cross-hatch pattern on the thick, fatty side of the breasts. Liberally apply salt and pepper deep into the opening.

In a large, ovenproof frying pan over high heat, sear duck breasts in canola oil, skin side down, for 2-3 minutes. Pour off fat from pan, a process called rendering. Continue cooking duck, skin side down, for 3 more minutes. Render fat again. Place frying pan in oven until breast is medium-rare to medium, about 8-10 minutes.

After duck is cooked, remove from pan and let rest before slicing.

Potato Salad

12 red or white nugget potatoes, blanched and cubed

4 strips smoked bacon or pancetta, diced

⅓ cup pine nuts (optional)

⅓ cup goat milk cheese

splash white wine vinegar

cracked black pepper to taste

1 bunch arugula or spinach

In the hot duck fat left in the pan, sauté potato cubes and bacon until golden brown. Add pine nuts, cheese, vinegar, greens, and pepper and cook until greens are slightly wilted.

To Plate: Place ¼ of potato salad in a ring mould. Slice duck breast. Remove mould from potato salad and fan duck slices atop potato salad. Squirt mustard sauce onto plate, making a design. Place nasturtium flower on top. Drizzle a little pistachio oil through mustard design to add another flavour dimension.

Beverage Pairing: Pinôt Noir

Smoked Paprika Chicken, Wild Mushroom and Chorizo Savory Bread Pudding, Sautéed Spring Beans, Oven-Dried Tomatoes, Red Wine Demi-Glace, Truffle Oil Drizzle

What can I say? This is chicken all dressed up. The spicy rich chorizo melds with the somewhat earthy wild rice in the bread pudding for a mosaic of flavours. The balanced bite of the smoked paprika red wine sauce and truffle oil puts this dish in the running for the "Last Supper"; this is one you'll want before you go to the electric chair.

Smoked Paprika Chicken

½ cup olive oil

1 heaping tbsp smoked paprika

salt to taste

2 Cornish game hens or baby chickens cut in half, backbones removed

Preheat oven to 400°F.

In a mixing bowl, combine olive oil, paprika, and salt. Toss chicken pieces in mix. Transfer to a large baking dish or roaster and cook in oven for 20 to 30 minutes.

Wild Mushroom and Chorizo Savory Bread Pudding

1 cup chorizo sausage

2 large whole eggs

½ cup whipping cream

zest of 1 orange, finely chopped

¼ cup fresh oregano, chopped

salt and pepper to taste

4 cups French bread, cubed

2 cups fresh crimini mushrooms, sliced

2 oz fresh morel mushrooms, sliced

1 tbsp butter

1 cup cooked wild rice (see page 16)

Preheat oven to 350°F.

In a baking pan, roast chorizo sausage for 10-15 minutes.

In a mixing bowl, slightly beat eggs into whipping cream to form a custard. Add orange zest, oregano, and salt and pepper. Toss in bread cubes. Set aside for 20 minutes to let the bread absorb custard.

In a saucepan on medium heat, sauté mushrooms in butter.

Chop sausage into slices. When bread has absorbed custard, mix in sausage, wild rice, and mushrooms.

Pack mixture into small, greased, parchment-lined ramekins. Cover with small rounds of parchment. Place in *bain-marie* (see page 21) and cook until set, about ½ hour, removing parchment in the last 10 minutes of cooking to brown tops.

Red Wine Demi-Glace

2 shallots, sliced

1 clove garlic, sliced

1 tbsp butter

1 tsp whole black peppercorns

1 sprig fresh thyme

1 sprig rosemary

½ 750-ml bottle dry red wine

2 tbsp balsamic vinegar

2 cups veal stock (see page 17)

1 tbsp cold unsalted butter

In a large saucepan on medium heat, sauté shallots and garlic in butter. Add peppercorns, herbs, red wine, and balsamic vinegar. Reduce liquid to ½ the original volume. Stir in veal stock. Reduce until liquid is a sauce-like consistency. Whisk in cold butter.

Sautéed Spring Beans

2 tbsp olive oil

12 oven-dried tomato halves (see page 16)

2 cloves garlic, minced

½ lb fresh spring beans

salt and pepper to taste

juice of 1 orange

In a skillet on high heat, heat olive oil. Add tomatoes and garlic and sauté for 1 minute. Add beans, salt, and pepper and sauté, tossing frequently, for about 3 minutes.

Squeeze orange juice over top.

To Plate: Cut pudding into desired shapes or cut 2 thinner pieces, and arrange beans in-between like a sandwich. Place chicken cut side down on pudding and beans. Pour sauce reduction over chicken to glaze. Sauce should pool slightly on plate. Drizzle with truffle oil if desired.

Serves 4

Beverage Pairing: Grenache or Grenache Blend

Oven-Roasted Lamb Sirloin, Pine Nut Praline Gremolata Crust, Potato Latkes with Spiced Yogurt Paneer, and Mint Chutney

This recipe came about when I decided I wanted to serve individual petits roasts of lamb. It's perfect when you want roast lamb but don't have the time. The sirloin is a beautifully tender, moist, and full-flavoured cut. The pine nuts caramelized under the broiler makes a wonderful crust, and the spiced paneer and crispy potato latke is a take on old-fashioned potato pancakes with sour cream. A bold, succulent, and impressive dish.

Potato Latkes with Spiced Yogurt Paneer

For Yogurt:

1 500-ml tub plain yogurt

pinch coriander seeds, toasted and ground

pinch cumin seeds, toasted and ground

pinch mustard seeds, toasted and ground

salt and pepper to taste

1 whole vanilla bean

For Potatoes:

4 russet potatoes

1 tsp coriander seeds, toasted and ground

1 tsp cumin seeds, toasted and ground

1 tsp mustard seeds, toasted and ground

1 tsp fennel seeds, toasted and ground

1 tbsp butter

2 tbsp olive oil

Drain yogurt overnight. The next day, season with spices. Cut vanilla bean lengthwise, scrape out seeds, add to yogurt, and whisk until incorporated.

Preheat oven to 350°F.

In a large pot, boil potatoes until only half cooked so that the starch remains to help form the cakes. Strain and let cool and then peel.

In a food processor fitted with the appropriate blade, blend potatoes until smooth.

In a mixing bowl, add the toasted and ground seasonings to the potatoes and form into small cakes.

In a large skillet on medium heat, heat butter and olive oil and cook cakes for 3 minutes on one side. Flip cakes, then place skillet in oven until latkes are warmed throughout and both sides are crispy, about 5-7 minutes.

Oven-Roasted Lamb Sirloin, Pine Nut Praline Gremolata Crust

1 cup pine nuts

3 cloves garlic

½ bunch flat leaf (Italian) parsley

zest of 1 orange

zest of 1 lemon

zest of 1 lime

2 tbsp brown sugar

2 8-oz lamb sirloins, cut into 4 4-oz petits roasts

2 tbsp olive oil

Preheat oven to 400°F.

In a food processor, purée pine nuts, garlic, parsley, zests, and brown sugar to make a paste-like mixture.

In a skillet on high heat, sear sirloins in olive oil on both sides. Remove from heat and coat with paste to make a crust. Place sirloins back in pan and bake in oven for 5 minutes or until preferred doneness.

Let rest for at least 5 minutes before plating.

Mint Chutney

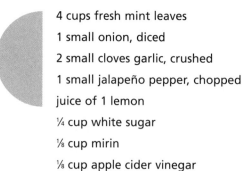

4 cups fresh mint leaves

1 small onion, diced

2 small cloves garlic, crushed

1 small jalapeño pepper, chopped

juice of 1 lemon

¼ cup white sugar

⅛ cup mirin

⅛ cup apple cider vinegar

In a blender, purée all ingredients to form a thick but smooth paste.

To Plate: Place latkes in centre of plate. Place lamb roast, unsliced, and with crust intact on latke. Put 3 little dollops of yogurt paneer around latke and dot with mint chutney.

Serves 4

Beverage Pairing: Cabernet Sauvignon

Moroccan Lamb Platter: Grilled Chops with Roasted Vine-Ripened Tomatoes Stuffed with Minted Couscous

4 vine-ripened tomatoes

1 cup couscous

juice of 1 lemon

2 tbsp extra-virgin olive oil

salt and white pepper to taste

water for boiling

¼ cup fresh mint, chopped

¼ cup fresh flat leaf (Italian) parsley, chopped

1 tbsp olive oil

4 1-inch thick lamb chops

salt and pepper to taste

1 sprig fresh rosemary

1 cup feta cheese (garnish)

your choice of mixed olives (garnish)

poppy seeds (garnish)

Preheat oven to 400°F.

Slice the tops off the tomatoes to expose flesh. Set tops aside. Remove flesh and seeds with a melon baller or large spoon.

In a large mixing bowl, combine couscous with lemon juice, 2 tbsp olive oil, salt, and white pepper. Pour in enough boiled water to cover. Place a sheet of saran wrap over the bowl to trap the steam and set aside for 4 minutes. When ready, fluff couscous and add mint and parsley.

Fill tomatoes with couscous and place tops back on. Drizzle with 1 tbsp olive oil and bake in a greased baking dish for 15 minutes.

Season lamb with salt, pepper, and rosemary. Grill lamb on medium heat for 3 minutes each side or sear in pan on high heat, 1 minute each side, and finish in oven for 5 minutes.

To Plate: Place 1 stuffed tomato in centre of plate, offsetting top of tomato to expose the couscous. Lean lamb chop against tomato. Place cubed feta and the olives at base of lamb and drizzle with the best quality extra-virgin olive oil. Top with poppy seeds and freshly ground black pepper.

Serves 4

Beverage Pairing: Malbec

Venison, *Petite Bel Paese* Fondue, Truffle Flour and Mushroom-Filled Agnolloti

What can I say about this dish? An instant can't-take-off-the-menu standout for a long time. Don't be afraid! Venison is a full-flavoured alternative to beef. Your taste buds will be rewarded. Or try ostrich as a substitute. Outstanding!

Petite Bel Paese Fondue
Roux + *Béchamel* with cheese = Fondue

For *Roux:*

¼ cup butter

¼ cup all-purpose flour

In a saucepan, melt butter and stir in flour until it is fully absorbed and has a golden colour. Set aside.

For *Béchamel:*

3 cups milk

½ onion, studded with 4 whole cloves

2 bay leaves

¾ cup Bel Paese cheese

salt and white pepper to taste

dash nutmeg

In a large saucepan, bring milk, onion, and bay leaves to a boil. Lower heat and simmer for 2 minutes. Strain milk, discarding bay leaves and onion.

Return milk to saucepan. Bring to a boil again. Slowly crumble in roux until combined. Add cheese and whisk until fully incorporated. Season with salt, white pepper, and nutmeg.

Pour fondue into 4 separate ramekins. Set aside until 20 minutes before serving time. Preheat oven to 400°F.

Place prepared ramekins in oven until cheese is bubbly, about 10 minutes.

Truffle Flour Mushroom-Filled Agnolloti

For Dough:

1 cup all-purpose flour

¾ cup truffle flour

3 egg yolks

1½ tsp truffle oil

For Filling:

5 cloves garlic, finely diced

2 shallots, finely diced

2 tsp extra-virgin olive oil

3 tsp unsalted butter

6 cups seasonal mushrooms, chopped

1 sprig fresh thyme

½ tsp sherry vinegar

¼ cup veal demi-glace (see page 17)

2 tsp heavy cream

Sift together the all-purpose and truffle flours.

In a food processor with dough blade attachment, blend eggs and oil. Add the sifted flour. Blend the dough until it comes together in a ball.

Remove dough and knead it into a smooth ball. Wrap in plastic and let rest for 30 minutes.

Roll out 2 sheets in a pasta machine to #6 thickness.

For Filling:

In a saucepan on medium-high heat, sweat garlic and shallots in butter and olive oil. Add mushrooms and thyme and sauté until half-cooked. Deglaze with sherry vinegar. When vinegar has cooked out, add veal demi-glace and cream. Cook until all the liquid has been reduced. Check seasoning. Set aside to cool.

To make Agnolloti, cut the pasta sheets into 3" squares. Place 2 tbsp of filling in centre. Brush edges with water, then place another square on top and seal the edges.

In a pot of boiling salted water cook Agnolloti until *al dente*.

Makes 10-12.

Venison

4 4-oz venison tenderloin pieces

Season with salt and pepper to taste. Grill on high heat, about 2 minutes each side, until medium-rare. Let venison rest after cooking.

To Plate: Put Agnolloti in one corner of the plate, the fondue in the other. Slice the venison on the diagonal and fan out.

Serves 4

Beverage Pairing: **Petit Syrah**

Argentinean Rib-Eye Steak with Wild Bacon Wrap, Potato Latkes, and Chimichurri Sauce

Chimichurri sauce is a traditional BBQ sauce of the "gauchos" in Argentina, a perfect accompaniment to any barbecued meat. We call the latkes "Oreo style" because the outside is crunchy like the cookie and the inside creamy like the filling.

Potato Latkes

1 chorizo sausage, diced

4 large russet potatoes

4 green onions, sliced

1 tsp salt

1 tsp ground white pepper

¼ cup yellow cornmeal

2 tbsp olive oil

2 tbsp butter

Preheat oven to 400°F.

In a large skillet, sauté sausage until cooked throughout. Drain fat.

Pierce potatoes with a knife several times and bake in oven until soft, about 1 hour. Cool for 10 minutes. Split potatoes in half, scoop out the cooked flesh, and press through a potato ricer.

In a large bowl, combine potatoes, sausage, green onions, salt, and white pepper. Mix well and form into 4 equal-sized cakes. Dredge cakes in cornmeal.

In a large ovenproof saucepan on medium heat, heat butter and oil. Add cakes and cook in the oven, turning twice until cakes are crunchy on the outside and soft on the inside.

Chimichurri Sauce

4 cloves garlic, peeled

1 bunch fresh cilantro

1 bunch flat leaf (Italian) parsley

½ tsp chile flakes

½ tsp black pepper

½ tsp salt

1 tbsp rice wine vinegar

zest of 1 lemon

zest of 1 orange

½ cup olive oil

In a food processor, blend all ingredients.

Argentinean Rib-Eye Steak with Wild Bacon Wrap

4 4-oz rib-eye steaks

4 slices of bacon (try wild boar bacon for change)

salt and black pepper to taste

2 tbsp olive oil

1 quail egg, fried sunny side up (optional) (to plate)

Wrap bacon around steaks and secure with a wooden skewer soaked in water. Lightly oil and season with salt and pepper to taste. On a skillet or grill on high heat, sear until medium-rare to rare, about 4 minutes each side.

To Plate: Put a heaping spoonful of chimichurri sauce in centre of plate and, using the back of the spoon, make a spiral that fits plate. Centre "Oreo-style" latke on spiral. Place steak on top and garnish with fried quail egg (optional).

Serves 4

Beverage Pairing: Zinfandel

Chianti Sun-Dried Tomato-Braised Veal Osso Buco, Applewood-Smoked Cheddar Risotto, Apple Juice-Glazed Fennel and Baby Carrots

Another twist on the classic Osso Buco, this dish boasts beautifully balanced fruit flavours and acidic components to give the demi a bright lively flavour. The vegetable component is somewhat of a classic pairing, but we replace the Parmegiano-Reggiano with Applewood smoked cheddar to elevate the dish to a truly mouth-watering palate pleaser. Full-on comfort!

4 1½"-thick veal shanks

½ tsp salt

½ tsp white pepper

¼ cups all-purpose flour

4 tbsp olive oil

6 tbsp unsalted butter

2 cups Chianti

4 cups veal stock

1 medium carrot, chopped into 3 pieces

1 medium white onion, quartered

2 ribs celery, cut in three

2 morita chiles

½ cup sun-dried tomatoes

1 tbsp whole allspice

½ cinnamon stick

2 garlic cloves, crushed

Preheat oven to 350°F.

Tie shanks with kitchen twine to hold them together. Season with salt and pepper. Dredge in flour.

In a large pan on medium heat, sear the shanks in olive oil and 4 tbsp of the butter until golden brown on all sides.

Transfer pieces to a large baking dish. Cover with Chianti and veal stock. Add remaining ingredients. Cover with foil and braise until shanks are very tender, about 2 hours.

Carefully remove the shanks from the braising liquid and keep warm. Strain the liquid, remove the sun-dried tomatoes, and discard the vegetables, spices, and peppers. Remove excess fat and reduce liquid until it is thick enough to coat the back of a spoon. Finish with 2 tbsp of cold unsalted butter.

Applewood-Smoked Cheddar Risotto

2 small shallots, chopped

4 tbsp unsalted butter

2 cups arborio rice

½ cup dry white wine

8 cups chicken stock, heated

½ tsp salt and ground white pepper

½ tsp white pepper, freshly ground

1 cup smoked Applewood cheddar cheese, grated

2 tbsp unsalted butter, melted

In a large saucepan, sauté shallots in butter. Add rice and stir to coat with butter. Stir in white wine and 2 cups of the chicken stock, and continue stirring until absorbed. Continue to add chicken stock, one cup at time, stirring slowly until the rice is creamy and *al dente*. Season with salt and white pepper. Remove from heat and stir in the cheese and butter.

Apple Juice-Glazed Fennel and Baby Carrots

1 fennel bulb, sliced in ⅛ thick rounds, top to bottom

12 baby carrots, scraped

2 tbsp butter

2 cups apple juice

1 cup chicken stock

salt and white pepper to taste

Preheat oven to 400°F.

In a large ovenproof saucepan on medium-high heat, sauté vegetables in butter until they are lightly browned. Stir in apple juice, chicken stock, and salt and pepper, and bring to a boil.

Remove and place pan in the oven until vegetables are tender, about 15 minutes. Remove the vegetables from the pan and keep warm.

Return pan to stovetop. Over medium heat, reduce the cooking liquid to a glaze and toss with the vegetables.

To Plate: Place about 1 cup of risotto in centre of each plate. Place veal shank on risotto without pressing down on rice. Pour sauce over top and frame risotto with 2 carrots and 2 fennel wedges.

Serves 4

Beverage Pairing: **Barbera**

Cheesecake with Banana Foster Sauce

A recipe I first made when I was about 10 years old – with my mom. We always enjoyed the dense but not overly sweet flavour of this particular cheesecake, which I have revised slightly. The Banana Foster Sauce is a stroke of genius. It transforms this easy-to-make cheesecake into an orgasmic dessert experience, transporting the tongue into a flavour realm reminiscent of your most memorable banana cream pie.

For Crust:

3 cups graham cracker crumbs

¼ cup white sugar

¼ cup unsalted butter, melted

½ cup chopped nuts or shredded coconut (optional)

For Filling:

5 whole eggs

1 cup white sugar

1 750-gram pkg plain cream cheese

1 250-ml tub mascarpone cheese

1 250-ml tub sour cream

½ cup white or dark chocolate, melted (optional)

½ cup your favorite liqueur (optional)

juice and zest of 1 lemon or orange (optional)

1 cup whipping cream

1 cup whole fresh berries or ½ cup puréed

Preheat oven to 350°F.

Place a shallow pan of water on bottom rack of oven.

In a large mixing bowl, combine all crust ingredients. Press into bottom and sides of a 10" round, non-stick, spring-form pan. Place pan on a baking sheet.

In a food processor, combine eggs and sugar. Add cream cheese, mascarpone, and sour cream. Blend until smooth. Stir in melted chocolate, liqueur, juices, and zest. Add whipping cream, but do not overwhip to avoid air bubbles. Add berries.

Pour filling into crust and place baking tray on middle rack of the oven. Bake until the cake has slightly risen over edge of pan and cracked at the edges, about 1 hour and 15 minutes. You may have to rotate cheesecake and check the water level in shallow pan.

Remove from oven and let cool to room temperature. Refrigerate at least 12 hours before serving.

Banana Foster Sauce

1 cup white sugar

¼ cup water

2 cups whipping cream

1 oz unsalted butter

2 each firm bananas, diced

2 oz dark rum

8 oz prepared caramel sauce, warmed

1 pinch salt

1 oz cold butter

In a heavy-bottomed saucepan on high heat, dissolve the sugar in the water, stirring until the liquid turns a caramel colour. Add whipping cream and whisk until sauce is syrupy.

In a saucepan pan on high heat, sauté bananas in butter about 2 minutes. Remove pan from heat. Add rum and return to heat, being careful of flare-ups; cook until flames subside. Stir in caramel sauce, salt, and cold butter. Keep warm.

To Plate: Place a cheescake slice on your favourite dessert plate and top with warm sauce. Save enough room for 2 slices. Trust me, it's gonna happen!

10-12 slices per cake

Beverage Pairing: Late Harvest Vidal

Toffee Coffee Pot de Crème

18 egg yolks

3 cups sugar

3 x ⅓ cup water

3 cups milk

3 cups cream

6 oz Kahlua

Preheat oven to 300°F.

In a mixing bowl, lightly whisk egg yolks and set aside.

In a heavy-bottomed saucepan on medium-high heat, dissolve sugar and water to make caramel.

While caramel is cooking, in a separate saucepan, slowly bring milk, cream, and Kahlua to a simmer.

As soon as caramel becomes dark and amber, carefully remove from heat and slowly pour the hot milk/cream mixture into caramel, whisking them together. Note: Because the caramel will bubble, it is best to do this step over the sink. Strain, skimming all the air bubbles, and refrigerate.

Pour 4 oz of liquid into clean ramekins. Cook the pot de crème in a *bain-marie* (see page 21) covered with foil, for 50 minutes. Only a nickel-sized centre should be jiggly when ramekin is shaken. The edges should be set.

Let cool. Wrap in plastic and refrigerate. The ramekins can be kept in the fridge for up to 4 days.

Beverage Pairing: **Tawny Port**

She's in Parties

Grilled Jumbo Scallops, Gazpacho Verde, Sweet and Sour Beet Salad

Gazpacho Verde

4 ripe avocados, roughly chopped

½ ripe honeydew melon, roughly chopped

2 kiwi fruits

1 jalapeño pepper, seeded (see page 16)

2 cucumbers, peeled and seeded

2 cloves garlic

juice of 1 lime

juice of 1 lemon

sea salt and white pepper to taste

⅛ cup extra-virgin olive oil

3 oz white wine (preferably Gewürztraminer)

2 cups edamame (soy beans), boiled and salted according to directions on package (garnish)

In a food processor or blender, purée all ingredients, except edamame, to a thick soup-like consistency. Season to taste. Set aside. The gazpacho can be made the night before.

Sweet and Sour Beet Salad

4 medium to large beets, peeled and cubed into ½-inch pieces

½ orange

6 cloves allspice

3 bay leaves

1 2-inch piece fresh ginger

⅛ cup apple cider vinegar

⅛ cup rice wine vinegar

¼ cup mirin

2 sprigs fresh tarragon, chopped fine

1 tbsp buckwheat honey

1 tbsp regular honey

2 tbsp sweet chile sauce

sea salt and white pepper to taste

Combine beet cubes, orange, allspice, bay leaves, and ginger. Cover with water and bring to a boil until *al dente.* Drain and let cool. Add apple cider vinegar, rice wine vinegar, mirin, tarragon, honeys, and sweet chile sauce. Season with sea salt and white pepper. Mix well. Marinate beets covered, overnight, in refrigerator.

Grilled Jumbo Scallops

1 tbsp unsalted butter

1 tbsp olive oil

16 large scallops

salt and pepper to taste

In a large skillet on high heat, heat butter and olive oil. Season scallops slightly with salt and pepper. Sear scallops until lightly caramelized and medium-rare, about 1½ minutes each side.

To Plate: Place beet cubes in middle of serving bowl. Pour 3 oz of gazpacho around beet cubes. Add 4 scallops to each bowl. Garnish with *crème fraîche* (see page 12) and drizzle a light ribbon of olive oil throughout. Dot with edamame.

Serves 4

Beverage Pairing: New Zealand Sauvignon Blanc

Clipped Living Greens, Hazelnut Wildflower Honey Vinaigrette, Cider-Poached Blue Cheese Salad

Summer on a plate: fresh, fresh, fresh. A simple vinaigrette that enhances, not masks, the beautiful and diverse flavours of new shoot greens. Here's where you get to support your local organic farmers and taste the eloquent and exotic fruits of their labour. Outstanding!

Hazelnut Vinaigrette

5 tbsp wildflower honey

1 tsp Dijon mustard

½ cup champagne vinegar

½ tsp salt

½ tsp ground white pepper

150 ml grapeseed oil

350 ml hazelnut oil

Using a blender, combine all ingredients except hazelnut oil. When well blended, slowly incorporate oil.

Cider-Poached Blue Cheese Salad

2 large Bartlett pears, peeled, cored and cut in half lengthwise

1 350-ml bottle strong apple cider

1 tbsp sugar

¼ tsp salt and ground white pepper

juice of ½ lemon

½ stick cinnamon

¼ tsp whole coriander seeds

Greens could be tatsoi, mizuna, baby New Zealand spinach, Lola Rosa lettuce, pea shoots, edible flowers, arugula, butter lettuce hearts, mustard greens, beat tops or leaves.

In a large saucepan on low heat, simmer all ingredients until pears are soft but not falling apart, about 10 minutes.

To Plate: Assemble a salad with your favourite seasonal clipped greens, or mesculin mixed greens. Slice or quarter pears and arrange on top. For a more substantial salad, add crumbled Stilton or gorgonzola cheese and toasted hazelnuts.

Serves 4

Beverage Pairing: **Australian Viognier**

Get-Naked Oysters and Granita

As we all know, oysters are thought of as the proverbial aphrodisiac, a form of culinary foreplay. They are also fun to feed to each other. There are many varieties of oysters, from strong to mild, briny to sweet. Smaller oysters such as Kushi, Kumamoto, or Malpeque are perfect for this dish. The granita, which is essentially a frozen flavoured juice concoction, is a nice accompaniment.

1 dozen fresh oysters

1 bottle champagne (to finish)

1 1-oz tin good quality sevruga caviar (garnish)

Simply shuck oysters, keeping all natural juice (referred to as liquor) in the shell. Make sure to detach bottom muscle so oyster will slide off shell.

For the granita, start with a simple syrup of 2½ cups of water with 1¾ cups sugar. Place mixture in pot and bring to a boil. Reduce heat and simmer until sugar is completely dissolved. This will act as a sweetener and give the granita the correct consistency. Herbs, such as basil or tarragon, would be a nice addition to infuse the simple syrup.

juice of 1 cucumber, peeled and seeded

juice of 1 lime

¼ tsp sea salt

1 cup simple syrup

In a shallow pan, mix all of the ingredients. Place in freezer. Remove every 45 minutes and rake mixture with a fork until completely frozen; it should be flaky and granular.

To Plate: Splash oysters with champagne and a dollop of caviar, *or* place 1 tsp of granita on each oyster and let slide!

Serves 4

Beverage Pairing: Dry, nutty Champagne

Deconstructed Whole Clam Broth "New England Style" Chowder with Smoked Scallop Potato Pavé

This dish makes a stunning presentation for what could be called soup for lack of a better term. It is based on New England clam chowder; however, all the elements are assembled within the dish as opposed to an actual combined soup. The Potato Pavé contains smoked scallops, Parmesan cheese, mascarpone cheese, and chives.

¼ cup carrots, chopped

¼ cup celery, chopped

1 white onion, chopped

1 tbsp unsalted butter

2 cups clam nectar

½ cup white wine

2 sprigs fresh thyme

2 bay leaves

1 *bouquet garni*

1 lb fresh clams, well rinsed

2 oz olive oil

4 6-oz halibut fillet

salt and pepper to taste

Preheat oven to 450°F.

In a saucepan on medium heat, lightly sauté carrots, celery, and onions in butter. Add the white wine, clam nectar, thyme, bay leaves, *bouquet garni*, and clams. Cook vegetables until *al dente* and clams have opened. Remove thyme, bay leaves, and *bouquet garni*. This is your soup broth; set aside.

In a large skillet on high heat, heat the olive oil until lightly smoking. Season halibut fillets with salt and pepper and place them presentation side down in pan.

Transfer to oven and roast for approximately 5 minutes. Carefully turn fillets over. They should be crispy and golden brown. Continue to roast until fish is cooked throughout, about 2 minutes.

Potato Pavé

1 cup mascarpone cheese

¼ cup grated Parmesan cheese

¼ cup fresh chives

1 tsp salt

1 tsp ground white pepper

8 large Atlantic scallops, cleaned

2 tbsp kosher salt

2 tbsp white sugar

2 cups cold water

8 large russet potatoes, peeled and thinly sliced

In a food processor, blend cheeses, chives, and salt and pepper until smooth and light green.

Place scallops in a mixture of the sugar, salt, and water and let brine for 1 hour. Drain and smoke lightly in home smoker (see page 24). Let cool, and slice each scallop into 4 equal disks.

Preheat oven to 350°F.

Cut sliced potatoes into circles to fit a 2 oz ramekin. Spray 4 ramekins with cooking oil and layer the potato disks, mascarpone and chive mixture, and scallops into each until the layers come up over the top.

Place ramekins in a deep tray and fill with hot water to come to ½ height of the ramekin. Cover the tray with foil and bake in oven for ½ hour or until potatoes are tender.

To Plate: Remove pavés from the ramekins by inverting them and place in individual serving bowls. Ladle clam broth and clams evenly around potatoes and top with roasted halibut fillet.

Serves 4

Beverage Pairing: **Chenin Blanc**

Pan-Kissed Ahi Tuna and Limoncello Risotto Cake with Spice Trade Sesame Pesto and Warm Ginger Vinaigrette

The combination of Italian risotto and Asian seasonings makes for a cross-cultural flavour explosion. A perfect way to enjoy blue-rare tuna is with the creaminess of the risotto and warm ginger vinaigrette. The beauty of the risotto cakes is that if you overcook the rice, it won't matter, and the cakes themselves can be made ahead of time, even the day before.

Warm Ginger Vinaigrette

90 grams candied preserved ginger, diced fine

1 cup virgin olive oil

½ cup rice wine vinegar

juice and zest of 2 lemons

juice and zest of 2 limes

juice and zest of 1 orange

1 tsp dried chile flakes

2 tsp togarashi

salt and pepper to taste

Mix all ingredients together.

In a small pot on medium heat, heat vinaigrette for 10 minutes before serving tuna.

Spice Trade Sesame Pesto

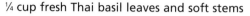

¼ cup fresh Thai basil leaves and soft stems

½ cup fresh cilantro leaves and stems

½ cup white sesame seeds

2 tsp wasabi paste

2 tbsp shiro miso

¼ cup rice wine vinegar

½ cup grapeseed or canola oil

¼ cup sesame oil

In a food processor, purée all ingredients. Set aside.

Pan-Kissed Ahi Tuna and Limoncello Risotto Cake

½ white onion, finely diced

1 tbsp canola oil

2 cups arborio rice

1 bay leaf

8 cups hot chicken stock (see page 18)

juice of 8 lemons reduced to ¾ cup
  or ½ cup Italian Limoncello liqueur

salt and white pepper to taste

28 grams mascarpone cheese

½ cup panko flakes

2 tbsp olive oil

4 4-oz pieces Ahi tuna

2 tbsp olive oil

Grilled Mushrooms

Brush 12 fresh shitake and 12 fresh oyster mushrooms with oyster sauce and lemon juice. Grill, or roast in a 400°F oven until softened and lightly wilted, about 15 minutes.

Preheat oven to 400°F.

In a saucepan on medium heat, sweat finely diced onion in canola oil.

Stir in arborio rice and bay leaf. Ladle in just enough hot chicken stock to cover rice. Keep stirring and adding hot chicken stock in small quantities until all the risotto is fully cooked. It is important to maintain a consistent temperature; risotto should be dry but sticky, with no excess liquid. Stir in reduced lemon juice. When all of the lemon juice is absorbed, season with salt and white pepper. Set aside to cool.

When cooled, form risotto into cakes. Insert 1 mascarpone ball into the middle of each. Dredge cakes in panko flakes.

In an ovenproof frying pan on medium heat, heat olive oil. Place risotto cakes in hot pan and cook until golden brown, about 1 minute. Flip cakes and place pan in oven for 5 minutes until cakes are warm throughout. Do this just before plating tuna.

In a skillet on high heat, sear tuna in olive oil until rare, about 1 minute each side. Slice.

To Plate: Place warm risotto cake in the middle of plate and surround with sliced tuna. Drizzle with 2 tbsp of the warmed vinaigrette and top with 1 tsp of pesto. Garnish with grilled mushrooms (see sidebar).

Serves 4

Beverage Pairing: **Pinôt Gris**

Lamb T-Bone, Smoked Gouda Potato Torte and Cinzano Demi-Glace and Spinach with Fresh Mint and Kalamata Olives

4 4-oz lamb T-bone steaks or double-cut chops

2 oz olive oil

8 sprigs fresh thyme, chopped

2 large shallots, sliced

1 tsp black pepper

1 tsp salt

juice and zest of 1 orange

Mix marinade ingredients together and pour over the lamb. Marinate at least 4 hours or overnight.

Broil in oven until medium-rare, about 5 minutes each side.

Cinzano Demi-Glace

4 oz Cinzano

½ cup veal demi-glace (see page 17)

2 oz cold unsalted butter

In a small saucepan on medium heat, reduce the Cinzano to ½, being careful not to let it flare up. Add the demi-glace and reduce slowly until it coats the back of a spoon. Whisk in cold butter.

Smoked Gouda Potato Torte

1 medium carrot, peeled and finely diced

2 ribs celery, finely diced

1 small white onion, finely diced

2 tbsp unsalted butter

¼ tsp salt

¼ tsp white pepper

2 cups smoked gouda cheese, grated

4 large russet potatoes, peeled and sliced thinly lengthwise on a mandoline

1 pinch salt

1 pinch white pepper

2 cups whipping cream, warmed

Preheat oven to 375°F.

In a large saucepan, sauté vegetables in butter, salt, and white pepper until slightly caramelized, then cool to room temperature.

In an 8-inch square, buttered, and parchment-lined cake pan, layer sliced potatoes, roasted vegetables, grated cheese, and seasoning, trying to make at least 8 layers. Finish top layer with grated cheese. Add enough warm whipping cream to come up almost the top of the potato layer.

Cover with tinfoil and bake for approximately 45 minutes, removing the foil for the last 10 minutes. Let rest for 15 minutes before cutting.

Spinach With Fresh Mint and Kalamata Olives

¼ cup olive oil

1 small clove garlic, minced

12 kalamata olives, pitted and sliced

1 lb fresh spinach leaves, stemmed, washed and dried

¼ lb fresh mint leaves

¼ tsp salt

¼ tsp white pepper

¼ cup apple cider vinegar

2 tbsp poppy seeds (garnish)

In a large saucepan, heat olive oil. Add garlic and olives and after 20 seconds add spinach and mint until spinach starts to wilt but not to cook. Toss with tongs. Season with salt and pepper and add cider vinegar immediately to dress. Do not pour excess liquid from pan onto spinach.

To Plate: Place spinach on plate and garnish with poppy seeds. Place a wedge of potato torte next to spinach. If lamb T-bone has been cut properly, the back end should be flat. Stand on flat end next to torte. Pour small pool of sauce at base of lamb.

Serves 4

Beverage Pairing: California Syrah

Beef Wellington and Roast Garlic Chive Mashed Potatoes

A modern twist on an old classic and a favourite at the Bins since day one. Feed it to staunch supporters of prime rib with Yorkshire pudding. Watch for a takeover bid from this new kid on the block. Oh yeah!

1 large portobello mushroom

olive oil

salt and pepper to taste

touch of balsamic vinegar

½ litre beef stock

3 tbsp pomery grainy mustard

⅛ cup unsalted butter

8 sheets phyllo pastry (see sidebar)

¼ cup unsalted melted butter

1 lb beef tenderloin tips, cut into 4 4-oz pieces

24 fresh spinach leaves, stems removed

1 whole roasted red bell pepper, peeled and seeded (see page 15)

1 cup sliced pecorino cheese

When working with phyllo, thaw in fridge overnight. Try to work quickly and keep reserved sheets covered with a damp kitchen towel. Butter between the layers to create flaky layers.

Preheat oven to 400°F.

Season portobello mushroom with olive oil, salt and pepper, and balsamic vinegar, and roast in oven until softened, about 10 minutes. Let cool, then chop into small pieces.

In a large saucepan on medium heat, reduce beef stock by ⅔. Sauce should be dark and thickened. Stir in mustard; do not boil once mustard is added. Finish sauce with butter until shiny and gelatinous.

Layout one sheet of phyllo and brush with melted butter. Fold it in half, side to side and brush again with butter.

In the centre bottom ⅔ of the sheet, place approximately 6 spinach leaves, one portion of tenderloin, and top with equal portions of mushrooms, red peppers, and cheese. Fold bottom edge of phyllo over top of filling. Press down gently. Fold over each edge and flatten out keeping the edges as straight as possible. Brush exposed phyllo with butter and roll into a small rectangular bundle.

Bake phyllo packages in oven for 3 minutes each side. Beef should be medium-rare and phyllo should be crispy and golden brown on both sides.

Roast Garlic Chive Mashed Potatoes

4 large russet potatoes, peeled and cubed

¼ cup unsalted butter

sea salt and white pepper to taste

¼ cup whipping cream

16 cloves roasted garlic (see page 15)

1 bunch fresh chives, chopped

In a large pot of salted water, bring potatoes to boil. Reduce heat to medium and let simmer until potatoes are tender enough to cut with a fork. Drain and return hot potatoes to pot. Add butter and sea salt and white pepper to taste. Using a whisk, begin to incorporate butter and break up potatoes with a whipping motion. When potatoes start to fluff and butter is fully incorporated, add cream and whip again. Potatoes should be moist and fluffy with minimal to no lumps. Using a spatula, fold in roasted garlic cloves and chopped chives. The secret to perfect mashed potatoes is whisking the potatoes while hot and not overworking, which will overdevelop the gluten and turn them into wallpaper paste.

To Plate: Cut each phyllo package in half on the diagonal; stand up on mashed potatoes and nape (drape) with sauce.

Serves 4

Beverage Pairing: **Classic Cabernet Sauvignon**

Erotic Chocolate Fondue and Dipping Doughuts

A very popular dessert at Bin 942; always an impressive conversation piece. I think it speaks for itself, so dip in, or use paint brushes and practice the ancient art of body painting. Nuff said. Amore till late.

Chocolate Fondue (Ganache)

6 oz good quality dark chocolate, chopped

⅓ cup heavy cream

1 tbsp butter

2 paintbrushes (optional)

Place chopped chocolate in a bowl. In a saucepan on medium-high heat, bring heavy cream with butter to boil and pour over the chocolate. Stir until smooth, if necessary warming over low heat.

Chill, without stirring, until firm. Ganache can be refrigerated 1 week, or frozen up to 3 months; just soften it in a tepid water bath before using.

To make a light Ganache: whip cooled Ganache until fluffy, 3-5 minutes.

Doughnuts

½ oz compressed yeast or 1 tbsp dried

¼ cup lukewarm water

½ cup milk

¼ cup unsalted butter

3 cups flour

¼ cup sugar

¾ tsp salt

1 egg, beaten

Dissolve the yeast in warm water.

In a pot on medium-high heat, heat the milk and butter until butter has melted. Let the liquid cool to lukewarm.

In a warm mixing bowl, sift the flour, add the salt and sugar, and make a well in the centre. Add the yeast mixture, milk, and beaten egg. Mix with your hands, gradually drawing in the flour to form smooth dough. If the dough is sticky, work in more flour.

Knead the dough as for firm doughs. Let it rise for ¾ to 1 hour.

Roll out the dough to about 1" thickness and, with a 3-inch cookie cutter, stamp out rounds. With a smaller cutter, stamp a round in the center of each one, creating 6 to 8 doughnut rings. (Discard centres.)

Transfer the prepared rings to a baking sheet or tray and let them rise until doubled in bulk, about 20 to 30 minutes.

In a deep-fat fryer, heat oil to 360°F. Gently lower the doughnuts into the fat, cooking just a few at a time. When done, doughnuts will float to surface and be golden brown.

To Plate: Place Ganache in fondue pot. Serve with doughnuts, hazelnut crusted bananas, fresh strawberries or seasonal fruits of choice, and marshmallows. For an extra bit of flavour, dust the doughnuts with a mixture of icing sugar and cinnamon.

Serves 4.

Beverage Pairing: Moscato d'Asti

Candied Apple Tart and Vanilla Ice Cream

It's a pie; it's a tart; it's a pie; it's a tart; it's bloody delicious. A cool version of apple pie/tart with ice cream, inspired by candy apples. Trick: roll ice cream in wax or parchment paper into pointy cone shape *à la* dunce cap. Refreeze in cone shape and remove paper when serving. Stand cone in middle of pie; dust plate with icing sugar.

Candied Apple Tart

For Applesauce:

¼ lb butter

2 tsp ground cardamom, toasted

2 cinnamon sticks, each broken in half

12 large yellow delicious apples, peeled, cored and cubed

4 tbsp wildflower honey

For Apple Slice Filling:

½ cup butter

2 cups sugar

6 cups water

1 lemon, sliced

6 large Granny Smith apples, peeled, cored and sliced lengthwise

1-2 sheets puff pastry

To make sugar glass, in a small saucepan, melt ½ cup sugar with a touch of water. Cook until lightly caramel in colour. Add 2 tbsp butter. Lay one 8½" x 11" sheet of parchment paper on the counter and spread sugar very thinly with an spatula. Let harden and break into pieces that are 3" x 3". The glass can be made ahead of time.

Preheat oven to 350°F.

In a large saucepan on medium heat, brown butter. Add cinnamon and cardamom. Stir in apples and honey. Simmer until it has a sauce-like consistency.

In another saucepan on medium heat, lightly caramelize sugar in butter. Carefully add water. Add lemon and bring to boil, then reduce heat and simmer for 5 minutes. This is your simple syrup.

Poach the Granny Smith apple slices in simple syrup until slightly tender. Remove and cool but save the syrup.

Cut puff pastry into circles and press into round moulds. Put ⅓ cup of applesauce in the bottom. Cover with sliced apple in a spiral pattern and dust with cinnamon and icing sugar. Bake in the oven until done, about 30 minutes. Brush pastry with melted butter 5 minutes before they come out of the oven. Leave oven on.

To Plate: Place a piece of sugar glass (see sidebar) over top of apple tart. Leave in oven for 3 minutes. The glass will wilt over apples, then harden again like *brûlés* or candied apples. It should crunch with a fork. Serve with vanilla ice cream.

Vanilla Ice Cream

Freeze 1 recipe of *crème Anglais* (see page 12) in an ice cream churn until slush. Add 1 cup heavy cream, lightly whipped, making sure to combine it thoroughly and continue freezing until the mixture is firm. Lift out the paddle. Pack down the ice cream. Cover churn tightly and store in the freezer. If chilling for more than 12 hours, let ice cream soften in the fridge for 30 minutes before serving.

Beverage Pairing: **Riesling Ice Wine**

Glossary

Achiote paste: made from the seeds of the annatto tree, it can be found in specialty markets.

Ancho chile: a dried chile, 3-4 inches long, reddish-brown in colour. In its fresh, green state, it is known as a poblano chile.

Asafetida powder: a traditional East Indian flavour enhancer. Use sparingly or the dish can become bitter.

Bel Paesse cheese: found in Italian or gourmet cheese shops. You can use French Port Salut as a substitute.

Blanch: to immerse food in boiling water for an instant, often followed by quick cooling in cold water.

Bonito flakes: dried and smoked tuna shavings. Available in Asian markets and most large supermarkets.

Braise: to cook food slowly in a small amount of liquid or fat in a covered pan on the stovetop or in the oven.

Caramelize: to heat sugar, or sugary foods, in a skillet on low heat until it turns brown and develops a caramel flavour.

Cassia buds: a type of cinnamon. Found in specialty markets.

Chinese five-spice powder: a mixture of five ground spices that usually consists of equal parts of cinnamon, cloves, fennel seed, star anise, and Szechuan peppercorns. Available in Asian markets and most supermarkets.

Chipotle pepper: a hot chile pepper with a dark brown skin and a smoky almost chocolaty flavor. Chipotles can be found dried or pickled and canned in adobo sauce. Found in Mexican markets and most large supermarkets.

Daikon: a large, white Asian radish. Available at most supermarkets.

Deep-fry: to cook food in hot fat deep enough to completely cover the item being fried.

Deglaze: to use a small amount of stock or wine to loosen browned bits of food on the bottom of a sauté pan and create base for a sauce to accompany the food cooked in the pan.

Edamame: Japanese for soybeans, they can be found fresh or frozen in Asian markets and most large supermarkets.

Flambé: to ignite warmed alcoholic beverages over food.

Guajillo chile: a dried red chile that is longer and narrower than most chiles.

Habañero chile: This distinctively flavored, extremely hot chile, is small and lantern-shaped. It ranges in colour from light green to bright orange when ripe.

Herbes de Provence: an assortment of dried herbs that commonly contains basil, fennel seed, lavender, marjoram, rosemary, sage, summer savory, and thyme.

Hominy: dried white or yellow corn.

Jalapeño chile: a smooth, dark green chile with a rounded tip. The seeds and veins are particularly hot. In their dried form, they are known as chipotles.

Jicama: a large root vegetable with brown skin and white crunchy flesh. Can be found in most supermarkets. Jicama is rich in potassium and vitamin C.

Kaffir lime leaves: used in Thai cooking and most readily available at Thai markets.

Konbu: dried seaweed used in Japanese dishes. Now available in most supermarkets.

Kosher salt: an additive-free coarse salt used in the preparation of Jewish cuisine and cooks who prefer its flavour.

Lemon grass: used in Asian cooking, it can be bought fresh or dried. Now available in most supermarkets.

Lily flowers: the delicate lily buds are available in Asian markets.

Mandoline: a compact, hand-operated machine with various adjustable blades for thin to thick slicing.

Masa harina: Flour made from dried masa.

Meyer lemon oil: Meyer lemons are specialty organic lemons. The flavour of the oil is a cross between lemon and tangerine. Found in specialty markets.

Mirin: a sweet Japanese cooking wine. Found in Asian markets and many supermarkets.

Miso: or bean paste, can be found in Japanese markets and health-food stores. It should be refrigerated in an airtight container.

Nori: thin sheets of seaweed found in most large supermarkets.

Panko flakes: lighter, fluffier bread crumbs used in Japanese cooking for coating foods to be deep-fried. Available in most large supermarkets.

Pasilla chile: a medium-hot pasilla that is blackish-brown in colour, and sold whole or in powder.

Pomegranate molasses: found in Lebanese markets, this molasses is high in potassium.

Purple potatoes: their skin colors range from lavender to dark blue, their flesh from white to beige with purple streaking. Available in gourmet markets.

Render: to melt solid fat to a liquid.

Ribena: a blackberry-flavoured drink found at specialty markets and some major supermarkets.

Rose water: a distillation of rose petals and a popular flavoring for centuries in Middle Eastern, East Indian, and Asian cuisines. Can be found in these markets and specialty food stores.

Sambal: a condiment served as an accompaniment to rice and curried dishes. Sambal oelek and bajak can be found in Asian markets.

Scotch bonnet chile: a small, irregularly shaped chile that ranges in color from yellow to orange to red. The Scotch bonnet is one of the hottest chiles and must be handled carefully (see **Basics**).

Sear: to brown surfaces of meat quickly to sear in juices. When searing meat, do not play with it. Simply place it in the hot pan. When meat is properly seared, it will lift easily, not stick and tear.

Sea salt: the result of evaporation from sea water, this salt is a bit more costly but is used the world over by gourmets who like its flavour and texture.

Sesame seeds: tiny, flat seeds that can be ivory or black. The black seeds are usually used for aesthetic reasons. Sesame seeds are available in supermarkets and can be found in bulk in Middle Eastern markets. They should be stored, airtight, in a cool, dark place for no longer than 3 months.

Stocks or demi-glaces: can be homemade (see **Basics**) or purchased from gourmet markets, fresh or canned.

Tahini: a paste used in Middle Eastern cooking, it is made of ground sesame seeds.

Tamarind paste/pulp: can be found in East Indian, Middle Eastern, and some Asian markets in jars or cans of pulp, paste, or ground into powder. Tamarind paste is one of the ingredients that give Worcestershire sauce its unique flavour.

Thai bird chile: a small and fiery chile that ranges in colour from green to red when fully ripe.

Tobiko: flying fish roe, often used in sushi or as a garnish.

Togarashi chile: a small, hot, red Japanese chile available fresh and dried. Also known as ichimi.

Truffle oil/flour: Black and white truffles are fungi that can grow up to a foot deep near the roots of trees. Their oils and flour can be found at specialty markets.

Zatar: a Lebanese seasoning found in Middle-Eastern markets.

Index

Index

Index

Index

Index

Index

Index